food
WITH
friends

food

WITH

friends

THE ART OF SIMPLE GATHERINGS

LEELA CYD

CLARKSON POTTER/PUBLISHERS
NEW YORK

For Cissy and Richard, my mom and dad

Copyright © 2016 by Leela Cyd

All rights reserved.
Published in the United States by Clarkson
Potter/Publishers, an imprint of the Crown
Publishing Group, a division of Penguin
Random House LLC, New York.
www.crownpublishing.com
www.clarksonpotter.com

CLARKSON POTTER is a trademark and
POTTER with colophon is a registered
trademark of Penguin Random House LLC.

Library of Congress Cataloging-in-
Publication Data is available upon request.

ISBN 978-0-8041-8709-1
eBook ISBN 978-0-8041-8710-7

Printed in China

Book design by La Tricia Watford
Photographs by Leela Cyd
Food styling by Ayda Rabana
Cover design by La Tricia Watford
Cover photographs by Leela Cyd

10 9 8 7 6 5 4 3 2 1

First Edition

CONTENTS

INTRODUCTION

The best food you will ever cook is simple, yet somehow special. It should only involve basic techniques, ingredients at their peak of freshness, and a touch of whimsy. Don't wait to plan a dinner party of complicated, unfamiliar, or fussy dishes; meals with friends can be a singular, delicious bite—like a tahini bun you've set in motion moments before (easy when you have a stocked pantry), a slice of blueberry mascarpone crostata (its rough edges are infinitely forgiving), or a salad mostly composed of flowers (everyone will gasp with glee). In our busy lives, where time is limited and digital connections take priority, preparing a small, delectable morsel and inviting a friend or two over to taste it (and linger) is a purposeful return to something tactile, sumptuous, and real—plus it's so much *fun*.

When it comes to creating happy memories, I believe more is more. So let's make these little moments happen, where we gather to celebrate the small stuff, the ups and downs, the ordinary and extraordinary, and set the table with our good china and thrift store glasses mismatching in imperfect harmony. And let's do it on a bright spring morning, a midweek night, or a Sunday afternoon. There's never a "perfect" time—so get started *now* with your joyful, tasty life!

If your intention, like mine, is to refine the art of hanging out, this book is for you. My collection of recipes and tips will show you how to turn an everyday necessity—eating—into an intentional gesture that sparks creativity, where a piece of toast can transport eaters across oceans to a bustling marketplace and a simple homemade soda bread bursting with candied walnuts, Turkish figs, and fennel will surely elevate your mood.

For whatever reason, I've always lived and breathed a messy, yet artful take on life: as a little girl I changed costumes five times a day (from ballet tutus to hand-me-down overalls), I hosted tea parties with all of my friends (both real and imaginary), and set the family table with loads of flowers plucked from our garden. I was born with an unrelenting need to lavish attention on my loved ones. My keenly observant parents channeled this interest by assigning me the task of planning and cooking feasts—both everyday and extravagant affairs—insisting I keep a journal of my menus and hiring me to bake for every holiday. Their crazy friends took me on as well, and I was merrily catering my first wedding at the age of seventeen!

My family and I followed a very basic philosophy—we kept our shared family dinners sacred. No matter the schedule-juggling of basketball practices, dance rehearsals, and my parents' demanding careers, we always stopped everything and ate together. As an adult, I realize the lasting impact that this daily ritual had on all of us: My brother, Nick, and I are now the lead cooks in our households. We just can't help ourselves—we find joy in feeding our friends, spouses, and, hopefully, one day our own kids.

When we were not at home eating together, my brother and I were lucky enough to travel the world as our photographer-dad's assistant. He and I took turns going along for the ride—Spain and Morocco instead of the last few months of third grade, Laos and Myanmar during Christmas break at age eleven, South India at sixteen, Tunisia and Rome while I studied history in my first year of art school. We saw the world and learned early on that food and laughter are a universal language and the most valuable currency for making new friends.

When I met my husband, David, in a performance art class, we immediately started saving for a lifetime of adventure. Dirt-cheap noodles and tacos taste pretty good when you have your eye (and belly) on Greece, the Netherlands, and England. We traipsed throughout these gorgeous countries, gulping down the art, culture, and food. Mutually bitten by wanderlust, we started to save up for living abroad for several months at a time: southern India, Vietnam, and Turkey.

Now I find myself traveling internationally for work teaching workshops and photographing hotels, chefs, and artisans. Between capturing images of each new locale, I seek out the grannies, the chatty shop owners, and the mustachioed uncles in the back of the hole-in-the-wall restaurants for cooking lessons. Spicy dahl with curry leaves and lime, sizzling sheep's cheese *pide* (pizza) in a brick oven, and mushroom spring rolls . . . . all are dazzling dishes I've learned at the side of someone who was "just cooking"—business as usual. Through these experiences, I learned that talking about food is the gateway to talking about anything. In about an hour (or sometimes within five minutes!), I get a window into another way of life: the gossip, traditions, hopes, and dreams are as exciting as the food is delicious.

This book is a collection of recipes I've gathered during my travels while shooting culinary stories and throughout my childhood in my family's sunny California kitchen. The six chapters, Breakfast & Brunch, Teatime, Happy Hour, Potlucks & Picnics, Desserts, and Tiny Takeaways, organize the recipes in the way I love to gather with friends using fresh, in-season ingredients whenever possible. (My emphasis for such is less on being healthy and more on expressing your creativity with food that *looks* and *tastes* good.) My hope is that my words, tips, and colorful images inspire you to live better in the moment and help you stop putting "have fun" on your to-do list.

It's experiences and laughs that matter most, not the most perfectly executed food, so relax a little, embrace the imperfect, and set off on a festive journey with fanciful tasty treats (just make sure to pack a few for the road).

SECRET INGREDIENTS

You never know who's going to stop
by or what last-minute friend fete you
may be invited to, so fresh, organic
produce, eggs, dairy, and good olive
oil are all important to have on hand,
but equally critical are the following
secret ingredients—flavor boosters that
quickly elevate simple cooking.

CHEESES

Always try to have one hard cheese such as Parmesan or Pecorino Romano, great for finely grating onto a kale salad or atop al dente pasta; one soft decadent ingredient to spin into a dessert (like cream cheese or mascarpone); and a solid salty Cheddar from Britain or nubbin of a French-style Comté to shred and scatter atop warmed lentils or to serve whole with jams and a baguette.

SALT

For eggs and toast, I go for flaky Maldon. Coarse Celtic Sea Salt is great to use on robust foods like roasted root veggies and potatoes (you'll love how this salt crunches in your mouth). Taha'a Vanilla sea salt from The Meadow perks up desserts like chocolate chip cookies. Jacobsen Salt, harvested off the Oregon coast, comes in brilliant flavors such as lemon, pinot noir, and smoked varieties.

NUT OILS

Roasted pistachio, hazelnut, and walnut oils from La Tourangelle in California are divine drizzled onto simple salads, soups, and roasted squash—even a teensy bit on ice cream sounds weird but is *delicious*.

PRESERVED LEMONS

While you can make these at home (check out Mark Bittman's recipe for Quick "Preserved" Lemons on the *New York Times* website), I find that picking up a few store-bought ones once a month from Whole Foods serves me just as well. There's nothing a small amount of these salty, umami-filled lemons cannot improve. Chop them up finely and mix them into a grain salad—you won't know what hit you.

HARISSA

This Tunisian chile paste is my go-to condiment for most things. With a subtle smoky spice and bold flavors from garlic, caraway, and coriander, it's fantastic with soft-boiled eggs and adds another dimension to a sauce or stew. You can make it yourself or buy DEA, the Tunisian brand (look for its beautiful, brightly colored packaging).

ASSORTED GERMAN MUSTARDS

I'd always been charmed by those adorable European mustard jars with their old-fashioned typography (perfect photo props!), and then I got hooked on the mustard's bright taste and instant zing. My favorite brands include: Löwensenf, Alstr (mustard in a tiny beer mug), Inglehoffer stone ground, and Thomy (mustard in a tube). Find them online or at local German delis.

AMARENA TOSCHI (ITALIAN CHERRIES IN SYRUP)

Transform an Old Fashioned cocktail or turn a milkshake into a rapturous moment! Available at Whole Foods and Italian groceries, a jar of these keeps well in the fridge for that "cherry on top" fix we all need sometimes. (Plus, the packaging is so cute!)

STYLE FILE

Setting your table can set your mood. When there's a stage for your sweet linen tablecloth, flowers from the garden, a favorite mismatched set of teacups, and secondhand silver, you cannot help but call your friends over to taste your latest creation. The beautiful food you've prepared deserves a special spot, and creating a cute atmosphere, a little act of caring for your guests, can be just as fun as cooking.

Let's talk about making your table pretty! In this chapter, I explore quick, inexpensive ways to doll up your own eating experience—from the unlikeliest of locations for sourcing tabletop accessories to taking inventory of heirlooms and acquiring a few special artisan-made items. All of these little gestures add up to a small collection unique to you that reflects your own taste.

SOURCING TREASURES

You don't need to be a millionaire to create happy tablescapes. If you focus on serving a pot of tea or a signature cocktail with just a few nibbles, you can allocate time to the other fun stuff: dressing your table in a way that's imperfect but looks like you. Here are a few sourcing tips:

1   **Scour thrift shops, yard sales, and estate sales.** Pieces worn and loved by others have a life of their own, and you're the lucky recipient: You get to add your personal touch to them for a little while before you pass them on a few years down the line. When shopping, keep your eye out for glassware, vintage pans, baking tins, and utensils.

2   **Traveling abroad?** Seek out ordinary shops instead of fancy tourist-trap stores. I've found some of the most adorable plates and cups in hardware stores in Italy and colorful dishes in restaurant supply stores throughout Argentina, Bali, and Thailand.

3   **Consider style before function.** Go for the color, shape, and texture that you want rather than something found in a kitchen supply store. A curtain on sale or a few yards of fabric can be had for a fraction of the price of a proper tablecloth. (No one will notice if it's unfinished.) Find marble tiles in home improvement stores to use as cheese platters and dessert trays (you'll only spend about five dollars instead of the fifty-plus a marble tray costs).

4   **Ask for family heirlooms.** Use what you already have (or what your mother or grandmother may be willing to pass down to you). My mother gave me her teacup collection from when she got married. A few cups have been lost over the years, but I still have some I use every day; they always remind me of her and make me smile.

5   **Find the work of artisans.** Buying a unique, handmade piece you are in love with—a coffee cup, a plate, or a bowl—is a great investment in "functional" art. Ceramicists, potters, and woodworkers are devoted to their trades, and supporting them by purchasing a coveted item adds a dynamic element to your table and a conversation piece for your guests.

SETTING THE TABLE

As a kid, I loved going overboard to set the table each night. I've dialed back that drama a bit now and landed at a happy medium. Opposite are a few tips to keep in mind.

The Overall Look When hosting friends, toss out the rules and go for a mishmash of plates, colors, and linens rather than a matching, coordinated look. It's easier to maintain. Think about it: If nothing goes together, then everything goes together (and it's *much* easier on you when a plate breaks). This is the way I shop: one plate here, another cup there, two little spoons that go together and six more that are all different. If this is too much, just keep everything white. You can still acquire items in a fun, treasure-hunting way—you just have a little art direction.

Place Settings If I'm hosting three or more people, I like to put a little something special on the plate—a single flower, a tiny card, or a lollipop or heavenly chocolate to pop into their mouths while I'm finishing our food. You want to give each guest a moment of delight that makes him or her feel special but that requires hardly any effort on your part.

Found Objects Keep your eyes open on your next hike. Your natural finds can be the most fun way to style a table and certainly a good conversation starter. The beach is one of my favorite places to "shop" for driftwood, seashells, and a bit of sea glass. When I lived in Portland, Oregon, I brought home pinecones, little rocks, and fir tips to put into a bowl for the middle of the table. When living in Brooklyn, I found the wackiest little picture frames, vases, and plates left by a curb and often threw them into the mix.

Flowers I like to arrange flowers two ways: I'll create a neighborhood bouquet, mostly from my property but a few little blooms or pieces of greenery from the public median and from outlying plants that hang over the sidewalk. (I assembled my wedding bouquet in this fashion!) Or I'll buy one bouquet from the farmers' market, trim the stems short, and separate all the blooms into their own little juice glasses or teacups.

Unscented Candles Add them with reckless abandon! I love cheap tea lights for their all-over glow—you can scatter them around the table on little dishes.

clearing the table

Whenever people are finished eating, I like to quickly clear the plates and put them into the kitchen sink to soak in warm water, and then I get back to my guests as quickly as possible. It makes the party last longer. The next morning, I'll just wake up a little earlier and do them while daydreaming about my next fete.

STYLING THE PLATE

Most of the time, I like to put out little plates—they always photograph better—and allow for a longer, more nosh-type of eating, with lots of tastes and helpings rather than one rigid meal. If served with garnishes like fresh herbs, toasted nuts, citrus wedges, and finishing salt and pepper, then whatever you've made will practically style itself. Be sure to have an assortment of toppings if your dish lends itself to that sort of thing. For example, soup looks so pretty when served with extra lemon slices, a drizzle of olive oil, and good crack of black pepper. The same can be said of oatmeal, which you can prepare and ladle out into bowls and guests can top with myriad fruits, seeds, a dollop of crème fraîche, and honey.

Skip any fussy styling. Food should look like food, with a very romantic, comfortable, and abundant sensibility. And so when plating something like a beautiful salad, I make sure that a few of the elements from the dish—like cheese and nuts in the salad, for example—appear at the top of the mound of veggies so guests know what flavors to expect. I do this by letting the ingredients gently drop from my hands from far above the plate, as if the ingredients are falling from the sky so that everything lands in an organic and unplanned manner. No need to apply each herb or seed with a pair of tweezers.

PHOTOGRAPHING THE FOOD

It's a golden time to be shooting. Capture the most sparkly food scene from your parties to make those no-shows drool:

- **BEFORE THE PARTY, PHOTOGRAPH YOUR FOOD IN NATURAL LIGHT.** Scoot your table or a pretty surface (like an old pan or cutting board) toward a window with indirect light and create your composition. The results will be so much better than working at night with a flash.

- **BRING IN COLOR, TEXTURE, SHAPE, AND SCALE.** Think like a painter and ask yourself: Is there enough variety of plates and glasses (shapes), is there a good mix of textiles and napkins (texture), is there a pop of vibrancy from the food or some nearby prop (color), and are there differences in size to keep the eye moving around the composition (scale)?

- **BREATHE LIFE INTO A SCENE WITH A HUMAN.** Nothing makes a table look more alive than some live action.

- **MIX UP YOUR ANGLES AND MOVE AROUND.** Don't just shoot food from above. Stand on a chair in the corner of the room or get really close and try to capture the little bits remaining on a plate. A good mix of wide, macro, and medium shots helps paint a full picture of your experience.

- **LOOK FOR SPONTANEITY *AROUND* FOOD.** Usually eating and drinking mean the coming together of friends, so be on the alert to shoot the life that exists around these moments—a "cheers" gesture or a friend at the stove—these shots are more compelling than a perfectly plated slice of semifreddo.

BREAKFAST & BRUNCH

rise and smile

The morning is my favorite time of day. I leap out of bed, usually
by 5:30, hungry for breakfast. This is the time when I'm at my most
creative, often gushing with lists of ideas over my daily cup of English
breakfast tea as I love the quiet optimism and sense of a fresh start
each sunrise brings. Growing up, I had to wake up or be left out—it was
that simple. It was never hard, though, especially on those occasions
when my dad delivered biscuits in bed that he served wrapped in tea
towels in a Dutch oven with a hot stone at the bottom of the pot to
keep the treats warm. Of course, he always had homemade jams and
salted butters at the ready—the guy is a pro breakfaster! And I learned
from the best.

While I enjoy being the beneficiary of a delicious morsel prepared for
me in the morning, it's even better to be the bearer of good edible
news in the form of Lemon-Lavender French Toast (page 46), Brûléed
Citrus Fruits with Fresh Herbs (page 27), or ingredients to make a
Spiced Strawberry-Balsamic Lassi (page 36). A home-cooked meal in
the early hours of the day is the quickest way to win someone's heart
(including your own!). When invited for brunch or a weekend stay, I
often arrive at my friends' homes armed with the right supplies—even
when they say they've got breakfast covered (another avocado tartlet
never hurt anyone).

Whether you're breakfasting or brunching with friends or taking a
moment on your own, you need to firmly push the daily restart button
to do it well. Its positive effects should not be underestimated (plus
think of all those carbs you'd be missing out on!).

Avocado & Coconut Tartlets, *page 20*

AVOCADO & COCONUT TARTLETS

MAKES SIX 4-INCH TARTLETS
OR ONE 9-INCH TART

In California and New York, fresh avocado smashed on hearty toast is the definitive "It Girl" breakfast—I've had humble avocado toast with friends in the comfort of their homes and paid a fortune for it in stylish cafés. I love the idea of elevating this hipper-than-hip breakfast into the fancy zone—a new twist on a predictable favorite. Inspired by the use of avocado in desserts in Vietnam and Brazil (hello, avocado milkshakes and ice cream!), I turned this creamy gem into a barely sweetened pudding and enveloped the shocking green filling in a classic pâte brisée crust. The results are a heavenly juxtaposition of opposites: elegant and cozy, healthful and decadent, sweet and savory. Confused skeptics will be bowled over at first bite. Serve with cups of piping hot black tea.

CRUST

1¼ cups all-purpose flour, plus more for the work surface

1½ tablespoons sugar

1 teaspoon fine sea salt

½ cup cold unsalted butter, cut into ¼-inch cubes

1 teaspoon distilled white vinegar

3 tablespoons ice water

AVOCADO CREAM

5 avocados (about 2¼ pounds), pitted and peeled

2 tablespoons whole milk

1 tablespoon lemon juice

¼ cup maple syrup

1 teaspoon vanilla extract

¼ teaspoon fine sea salt

⅓ cup unsweetened coconut flakes, lightly toasted, for garnish

MAKE THE CRUST: In a food processor, mix the flour, sugar, and salt together. Pulse the butter into the flour mixture in 3 to 4 short bursts, until the mixture resembles coarse meal. In a small bowl, mix the vinegar with the ice water, then drizzle over the flour mixture. Pulse a little more until the crust just clumps together. Turn the dough out onto a lightly floured surface and squeeze together to become a ball. Knead about 3 times to create a 4-inch round disk. Wrap in plastic wrap and refrigerate for 1 hour, to allow the gluten in the flour to relax.

Lightly flour your surface and pound the dough out flat with a rolling pin to soften it and make it workable. Roll the dough into a large ¼-inch-thick rectangle. If making individual tartlets, cut the dough into 6 rough pieces, each about an inch wider on all sides than your removable bottom tartlet pans. If making a 9-inch tart (see Note, page 21), roll the dough out a little larger than the pan. Lay each piece of dough gently into a pan, taking care not to stretch or pull the dough. Lightly press into the bottom and sides of the pans, then use a rolling pin to roll off the excess dough from the edges of the pans. Gently poke the tart bottoms with a fork about 5 times. Place the crusts in the freezer and let sit for about 1 hour.

Preheat the oven to 375°F.

Remove from the freezer and place the tartlet shells on a baking sheet and bake for about 15 minutes, or until the crusts are golden brown and fragrant. Transfer the tartlet shells to a wire rack to cool to room temperature.

MAKE THE AVOCADO CREAM: Just prior to serving, in a food processor or blender, combine the avocados, milk, lemon juice, maple syrup, vanilla, and salt. Blend until the consistency is airy, smooth, and light.

Use a spatula to transfer the cream to a zip-seal plastic bag and snip ½ inch off a bottom corner to make a piping bag. Gently pipe the cream onto each shell (½ to ¾ cup cream per tart) in a circular motion, starting with the perimeter of the tart shell and working in to the center—you can get as fancy or rustic as you'd like. Serve immediately, garnished with the coconut.

note The 9-inch tart option makes this breakfast easy to serve to a crowd, although preparing it ahead of time proves tricky as the avocado oxidizes fast. If you must prepare ahead, put the avocado cream in a bowl with a thin sheen of water drizzled over the top. Cover with a sealed lid and refrigerate for no more than 2 days. When ready to use, tip the water out, stir, and transfer the filling to a zip-seal plastic bag for filling the tart.

BIRCHER MUESLI WITH PLUMS & BLACKBERRY MASH

SERVES 4

When the warmer months are in full swing, with their golden mornings and early sunrises, I love to reach for a bowl of nourishing muesli. It's filling and delicious, and can be adapted according to what fruit is available. This version is my favorite to serve on long summer weekends with the girls or to take along to a brunch party. Most of this delicious mixture gets made the night before, with little blackberry layers added at the last minute. The muesli is dotted with fresh plums and dried figs and layered with mashed blackberries—and really celebrates that late-summer headiness when all the berries are still in full flush and the stone fruits are so sweet they're practically oozing with natural sugars.

1 cup rolled oats

⅓ cup slivered almonds, plus more for garnish

2 tablespoons chia seeds

Generous pinch of fine sea salt

1 dried Turkish fig, roughly chopped

1 cup whole milk

½ cup plain whole-milk yogurt

1 teaspoon vanilla extract

1 tablespoon honey

1 medium apple, shredded on a box grater (about 1 cup)

2 cups blackberries

4 fresh medium red plums, quartered and thinly sliced

Bee pollen, for garnish

In a small bowl, mix together the oats, almonds, chia seeds, salt, and chopped dried fig. In a large bowl, whisk together the milk, yogurt, vanilla, and honey. Pour the oat mixture into the milk mixture and stir thoroughly to combine. Cover with plastic wrap and refrigerate for at least 6 hours, or overnight.

When ready to serve, stir ¼ cup water into the muesli. Add about half the shredded apple and stir. In a medium bowl, gently mash 1½ cups of the blackberries.

In the bottom of a small jam jar or pretty glass, spread about 1 heaping tablespoon of the blackberry mash. Layer 2 heaping tablespoons of the muesli, add 1 more heaping tablespoon of the blackberry mash, followed by 2 heaping tablespoons of the muesli. Top with a generous pinch of the remaining shredded apple, a couple of whole blackberries and the slices of one plum. Garnish with a few slivered almonds and a little bee pollen. Repeat this layering process with the remaining three portions. Serve immediately, or cover and keep in the fridge for up to 3 days.

1

2

3

4

5

6

7

8

9

STEEL-CUT OATS WITH TOPPINGS

SERVES 2

I am a porridge nut—it's so nourishing and cozy, and so full of potential variation. For me, a great bowl of oatmeal depends on the proper toppings: I like different textures, flavors, and even temperatures. Feel free to change this recipe based on season, weather, and your appetite in any specific moment. Once you master this mindset, you'll never think of oatmeal as a boring, ho-hum breakfast—rather it's a canvas in which you can make your mark, and set the tone for the rest of your day.

OATS

1 tablespoon unsalted butter

1 cup steel-cut oats

1½ cups almond milk or whole dairy milk

¼ teaspoon fine sea salt

1 teaspoon vanilla extract

¼ teaspoon ground cinnamon

¼ teaspoon ground ginger

1 tablespoon ground flaxseeds

TOPPINGS

1 cup chopped fresh fruit

½ cup chopped toasted nuts

¼ cup toasted unsweetened shredded coconut

¼ cup roughly chopped dried fruit (such as figs or apricots)

2 tablespoons sesame, pumpkin, or hemp seeds

2 tablespoons rich dairy, such as whole-milk yogurt or sour cream

2 tablespoons nut butter (such as cashew, peanut, or almond)

Flaky sea salt, to taste (such as Maldon or Taha'a Vanilla salt)

Warm maple syrup, honey or brown sugar, to taste

COOK THE OATS: In a medium pot, melt the butter over medium heat. Add the oats and cook, stirring occasionally, until the oats produce a toasty, popcorn-like aroma, about 5 minutes. Add the milk, salt, and 1½ cups water. Bring the liquid to a boil, then reduce to a simmer and cook the oats, stirring occasionally to scrape up the oats from the bottom of the pot, for about 20 minutes longer, until cooked through but still a little toothsome. Stir in the vanilla, cinnamon, ginger, and ground flaxseeds. Cover the pot, remove from the heat, and let stand for 3 to 5 minutes.

SERVE THE OATS: Ladle the oatmeal into 2 bowls. Arrange the toppings as desired in each bowl and serve immediately.

1. The Tropics (coconut, pineapple, passion fruit, and cashews)
2. Americana (blueberries, strawberries, yogurt, and bee pollen)
3. The Cozy (apple slices, cranberries, almonds, and cinnamon)
4. Viva Mexico (pear, pepitas, dates, and chile)
5. The Crunch (granola, sunflower seeds, and shredded coconut)
6. The Health Nut (blackberries, toasted walnuts, and flax seeds)
7. The Greek (dried figs, pomegranate seeds, pistachios, and Greek yogurt)
8. The Sexy (plums, dark chocolate, dried cherries, and honeycomb)
9. The Childhood Special (whole milk, peanut butter, strawberry jam, and banana)

BRÛLÉED CITRUS FRUITS WITH FRESH HERBS

SERVES 4 TO 8

2 grapefruits

2 blood oranges

2 oranges

2 tangerines

¼ cup turbinado sugar

1 tablespoon grated lemon zest

½ teaspoon Taha'a Vanilla sea salt (see page 9) or fine sea salt

2 sprigs fresh tarragon, leaves roughly chopped

½ cup fresh mint leaves, roughly chopped

Baking citrus is new to me, but once I started, I could hardly stop—the sweet/tart concentrated flavors are addictive! As a kid I loved eating Starburst, WarHeads, and all manner of sour sugar candies (maybe I was a masochist, but I loved the hair-bending pain of the sour flavor). So here I've come full circle, but in a much healthier fashion. These aromatic broiled citrus are sweet, a touch tangy, and verdant with the smattering of fresh mint and tarragon. This simple recipe truly is greater than the sum of its parts.

Preheat the oven to 400°F. Line a baking sheet with parchment paper.

Halve each piece of fruit (see Note) along the equator of the fruit. Slice a tiny bit off the bottom of each fruit, so they will sit upright. With a sharp paring knife, score along the perimeter, where the flesh and membrane meet. Score each segment along the white membrane casing as well, so each segment of fruit will be easy to scoop out after roasting.

Place the fruit cut-side up on the prepared baking sheet and bake for about 10 minutes, to allow the flavors to concentrate. Remove from the oven and turn the broiler to high. Evenly sprinkle the turbinado sugar over the fruit. (Distribute the sugar as evenly as you can, using a little more on the grapefruits, a little less on the smallest tangerines.) Broil for 2 to 3 minutes, until a little char is visible and the sugar is melted.

In a small bowl, combine the lemon zest, vanilla salt, and chopped herbs. Just before serving the broiled citrus, top each with a little of the herb mixture.

note Buy whatever seasonal citrus you can and use it for this recipe—tangerines, blood oranges, regular oranges, grapefruits, it's all good. Where I live, I have access to a range of citrus year-round (grown organically in nearby Ojai), but you may not. So use what you've got; you won't be disappointed.

When I was eleven years old, my father and I explored Myanmar for three weeks, my dad photographing temples and long-forgotten spaces as I trailed behind him, carrying his camera equipment and my journal. We then drove across the border to Laos to embark on a 230-mile journey down the Mekong River. Watching each sunset and sunrise glisten in colors I never could have dreamed up, we held tight to each other's hands—it's a memory not easy to forget. Nor were the *bananas on fire,* a dish I dared order at our little jungle hut hotel on the riverbank in Luang Prabang.

I now realize that those fiery bananas were no more than the vaguely French dessert *bananes flambées,* but its Laotian translation was far more exciting. My version is less sweet than the classic (Laos bananas are sweeter than anything we can get in the United States) but uses a few crushed banana chips for texture and maximal banana flavor.

BANANAS ON FIRE
SERVES 4

TOPPING

¼ cup crème fraîche

½ cup heavy (whipping) cream

1 tablespoon powdered sugar

Pinch of salt

BANANAS

3 tablespoons unsalted butter, sliced

⅓ cup packed dark brown sugar

¼ teaspoon freshly grated nutmeg

¼ teaspoon fine sea salt

1 vanilla bean, halved lengthwise

4 medium bananas, quartered

2 tablespoons rum (brandy or orange liqueur would work well, too)

⅓ cup lightly crushed banana chips

MAKE THE TOPPING: In a bowl, with an electric mixer, whisk the crème fraîche, heavy cream, powdered sugar, and salt until stiff peaks form. Cover and refrigerate until ready to serve.

COOK THE BANANAS: In a large skillet, melt the butter over medium heat. Stir in the brown sugar, nutmeg, and salt. Scrape in the vanilla seeds and add the pod, too, and cook until melted and smooth, stirring constantly, about 4 minutes.

Increase the heat to high and add the bananas, stirring to coat in the sugar mixture. Remove the skillet from the heat and pour the rum (see Note) into one side of the skillet. Using a long lighter or long match, quickly ignite the alcohol mixture—the flames will be quite large, so step away from the burner with the pan in your hand until the fire goes out. Return the pan to the burner for about 2 minutes, shaking the bananas slightly to evenly coat.

Pour the bananas onto 4 small plates and garnish with a dollop of the crème fraîche topping and a tablespoon of crushed banana chips. Serve immediately.

note For safety's sake, never pour alcohol directly from the bottle into a hot pan. Instead, decant the alcohol into a cup measure with a spout, so you have more control over the stream of alcohol into the pan. Keep a lid nearby, in case the flames get unruly.

APPLE FRITTERS & CINNAMON YOGURT CREAM

MAKES ABOUT 12 FRITTERS

Making fried food at home is a treat not to be sniffed at—it's a bit of a production, but when it's right, it's just sublime. These apple fritters are no exception to the heavenly category: puffy with a cream-laden crust, soft and yielding with a melty apple center, they are what apple pie aspires to be! With a dollop of cinnamon cream and a dusting of cinnamon sugar, these fritters are the perfect meal for a crisp, sunny morning.

CINNAMON YOGURT CREAM

1 cup plain whole-milk Greek yogurt

1/3 cup powdered sugar, sifted

1 teaspoon ground cinnamon

1 teaspoon vanilla extract

Pinch of salt

FRITTERS

1/2 cup plus 2 tablespoons granulated sugar

3/4 teaspoon ground cinnamon

1 cup whole milk

1 cup heavy (whipping) cream

4 teaspoons vegetable oil, plus extra for frying

2 large eggs, lightly beaten

2 cups all-purpose flour, plus a little more for dredging

2 teaspoons baking powder

1/2 teaspoon fine sea salt

4 medium Granny Smith apples, cored, peeled, and cut into 1/2-inch-thick rings

MAKE THE CINNAMON YOGURT CREAM: In a large bowl, whisk together the yogurt, powdered sugar, cinnamon, vanilla, and salt until the sugar has dissolved. Cover and chill the cream until ready to serve.

MAKE THE FRITTERS: In a medium bowl, combine 1/2 cup of the granulated sugar and the cinnamon. Line a baking sheet with paper towels.

In another medium bowl, whisk together the milk, cream, 4 teaspoons of the oil, and the eggs. Stir in the flour, baking powder, salt, and remaining 2 tablespoons granulated sugar until you have a smooth batter.

In a large, heavy, high-sided skillet, heat 2 inches of vegetable oil until it reaches 375°F on a deep-fat or candy thermometer, and a drop of batter into the oil makes it bubble rapidly.

Dredge the apple slices in a little bowl of flour and then in the batter until all sides are coated.

Working in batches, fry the apple slices until golden brown, about 4 minutes per batch, flipping them halfway through (I like chopsticks for flipping the fritters). Transfer the finished fritters to the lined baking sheet and continue frying. Toss the fritters in the cinnamon sugar mixture and serve hot, with the cream.

This breakfast board doesn't have a strict procedure; it's more a formula for improvisation. More important than having the exact ingredients that you see here (though these are all great pantry and fridge staples) is for you to grasp the overall concept of serving several flavors (sweet and savory), textures, and delights in a quick and easy way. If you have guests sleeping over, you'll find them positively squealing with delight when you knock on their door and serve this as breakfast in bed, especially when accompanied by a pot of tea or steaming hot French press. This recipe is proof that you don't have to do something overly complicated or even spend time at the stove to really make friends feel special. It's the perfect way to eat and relax, converse and be leisurely.

ANYTHING-GOES BREAKFAST BOARD

SERVES 2

2 slices hearty German-style brown bread, cut into triangles

4 slices baguette

1 semihard salty cheese such as Piave Vecchio, Comté, or Gruyère, cut into 8 long spears ¼ inch thick

4 large cubes of your favorite cheddar cheese

1 soft cheese such as fresh goat cheese, Boursin, burrata, or even a quality cream cheese

½ cup pitted briny green olives

½ cup Quick Pickled Shallots (page 123)

2 types of jam, 1 to 2 tablespoons of each

2 tablespoons unsalted butter, slightly softened

Flaky sea salt (Maldon is easiest to find)

2 large hard-boiled eggs

2 pieces seasonal fruit, cut into slim wedges or bite-size pieces

Freshly ground black pepper

Gather your two prettiest platters or cutting boards and set at the ready. Divide the cut breads and cheeses between the platters. Place the olives and shallots in their own small bowls, and spoon the jams into small vessels (shot glasses are surprisingly lovely here). Smear the butter in a dollop onto the board and sprinkle with a touch of flaky salt. Nestle the hard-boiled eggs and cut fruit onto the board anywhere you think it looks pretty. The presentation can be as natural and wild or contained and orderly as you like. Serve with butter knives and a napkin, along with extra salt and pepper.

ROASTED PLUMS WITH BURRATA

SERVES 4 TO 6

Simple is sexy—and this idea of fruit and luscious dairy is so sexy it hardly needs an introduction, let alone a recipe. Buying a bag of burrata is like owning an eight-dollar lump of Gastro-Gold: Upon opening this oozy, creamy cousin of fresh mozzarella, you'll attract fans you didn't know you had. It's a dangerous game, this fresh Italian cheese thing, so just be careful to whom you expose this ridiculous platter of cheese and seasonal fruit—he or she may get burrata fever and never recover.

8 medium plums, halved (see Note)

2 tablespoons olive oil

2 tablespoons light brown sugar

⅛ teaspoon fine sea salt

1 package (8 ounces) burrata cheese

Honey, for drizzling

¼ cup walnuts, crushed, for garnish

Preheat the oven to 425°F. Line a baking sheet with parchment paper.

In a large bowl, gently toss the plums, olive oil, brown sugar, and salt together with your hands, being careful not to bruise the fruit. Spread on the prepared baking sheet and roast for about 10 minutes, depending on how big your fruit halves are, until the fruit is golden brown along its edges and its flesh has softened when pricked with a fork.

Place the burrata cheese in the middle of a big platter and make a few cuts into the center, removing a tiny wedge before serving (this helps the contents ooze out). Using tongs, place the roasted, still-warm fruits on and around the mound of cheese. Drizzle a tiny bit of honey over everything. Garnish with the crushed walnuts sprinkled evenly over the top. Serve immediately.

note If plums are not in season, you could use any juicy, local fruit in their place. A platter of roasted pears, sautéed apples, or even seared figs would be divine in this recipe.

SPICED STRAWBERRY-BALSAMIC LASSI

SERVES 4

Lassi is a catchall term in India, Pakistan, and Bangladesh, referring to any drink consisting of blended yogurt, spices, and often fruit (there are even savory lassis with loads of salt). Inspired by my friends Kim and Tyler Malek at Salt & Straw ice creamery in L.A. and Portland, I re-envisioned one of their most popular flavors—honey balsamic strawberry with cracked pepper—in lassi form. The play of tang, sweetness, and subtle spice is refreshing and exciting. The rosy pink ballerina hue is enough to get anyone dancing with jazz hands and pencil turn–pivot–fan kick all while bumping to Madonna's "Material Girl" at high volume. What has your breakfast beverage done for you lately?

2 cups sliced strawberries, plus 4 pretty strawberries for garnish

1 cup whole milk

1 cup ice cubes

2/3 cup plain whole-milk yogurt

1 tablespoon balsamic vinegar

1 tablespoon honey

1 medium date, pitted and roughly chopped

1 teaspoon vanilla extract

¼ teaspoon ground cardamom

¼ teaspoon freshly ground black pepper

In a blender, combine all the ingredients and blend until smooth. (This takes me about 1 minute in my high-speed Vitamix blender, but may take a little longer depending on your appliance.)

Pour into 4 pretty juice glasses and garnish with strawberries.

IRISH SODA BREAD WITH RUM-PLUMPED FIGS & CANDIED WALNUTS

MAKES 2 LOAVES

Soda bread is a soul soother—it humbly straddles the divide between wholesome and decadent. I first encountered this craggy breakfast treat when my family traveled to Ireland. It poured every day and my brother and I moped (as only teenagers can do!), bemoaning the loss of our summer.

The silver lining of our trip was the soda bread each morning. Each B&B host made hers slightly differently, sometimes with bits of fruit and various spices and nuts, other times pure and simple. My take involves the flavors of California, and this recipe makes two loaves, so you can gobble one up and gift the other to a friend.

½ cup rum

1 cup dried Mission fig slices (¼-inch disks; about 18 whole figs)

1 tablespoon unsalted butter, plus more for serving

¼ cup packed light brown sugar

1 cup walnuts, slightly chopped

4½ cups all-purpose flour (plus more for kneading the dough)

3 tablespoons granulated sugar

1 teaspoon baking powder

1 teaspoon baking soda

1¾ teaspoons fine sea salt

1 tablespoon fennel seeds

1¾ cups buttermilk

2 tablespoons canola oil

1 large egg

Jam, for serving

Preheat the oven to 375°F. Line a baking sheet with parchment paper. In a medium saucepan, bring the rum to a boil. Add the sliced figs, cover, remove from the heat, and let steep for about 10 minutes. Drain off and discard the rum and set the figs aside.

In a medium skillet, melt the butter and brown sugar over medium-low heat. Add the walnuts and stir constantly, browning the nuts until they smell toasted, 4 to 5 minutes. Spread the walnuts on a plate to cool and harden.

In a large bowl, whisk together the flour, granulated sugar, baking powder, baking soda, salt, and fennel seeds. In a medium bowl, whisk together the buttermilk, oil, and egg. Create a well in the flour mixture and pour the buttermilk mixture into the well. Incorporate the wet mixture into the dry with a spatula, giving it a few quick stirs, until the dough just comes together. Turn it out onto a well-floured counter, knead ever so slightly to form a large smooth ball, and slice in half to create 2 circular loaves.

Place the loaves on the lined baking sheet. Score an X in the top of each loaf with a sharp paring knife and dust the loaves with flour. Bake for about 40 minutes, or until the crust is very golden. Transfer to a wire rack to cool. Serve at room temperature or slice and serve toasted with butter and jam.

CHOCOLATE MARCONA MINI MUFFINS

MAKES 24 MINI MUFFINS

1¼ cups all-purpose flour

½ cup almond meal

½ cup unsweetened cocoa powder (I like Scharffen Berger or Valrhona for depth of flavor)

2 teaspoons baking powder

½ teaspoon baking soda

½ teaspoon salt

1 cup buttermilk

½ cup packed light brown sugar

⅓ cup vegetable oil

1 large egg

1 teaspoon vanilla extract

⅔ cup Marcona almonds (see Note)

¾ cup chocolate melting wafers

These mini muffins received the highest form of praise: They were approved by Amelia and Deckard, the two kids of my dear friend. (They were even caught stealing away with a few, so they could share "the brownies" with their friends when their mom wasn't looking.) These muffins veiled as brownies are tasty and somewhat wholesome, with a low sugar content and the addition of protein-packed almond meal. They make a great road trip snack and/or pair perfectly with a strong coffee as a whimsical, chocolaty breakfast treat.

Preheat the oven to 375°F. Grease 24 cups of mini muffin pans or line with mini muffin liners.

In a large bowl, sift together the flour, almond meal, cocoa powder, baking powder, baking soda, and salt. Discard any large lumps of almond meal remaining in your sifter.

In a medium bowl, whisk together the buttermilk, brown sugar, vegetable oil, egg, and vanilla until the mixture is uniform. Fold the buttermilk mixture into the flour mixture, stirring just until the batter comes together. Gently fold in ⅓ cup of the almonds and the chocolate wafers into the batter.

Scoop a heaping tablespoon of batter into each muffin cup. Top with the reserved ⅓ cup Marcona almonds, pressing the almonds gently into the top of the batter so they don't pop out while baking.

Bake the muffins for 12 to 15 minutes, until a toothpick inserted in a muffin comes out clean. Let cool for 5 minutes in the pan, then gently remove the muffins and let them finish cooling on a wire rack.

note Marcona almonds are indeed more expensive than regular almonds. They have a salty decadence to them that is very distinctive. If you'd rather make your own, just toast raw almonds in a bit of olive oil over medium heat and sprinkle generously with flaky salt.

My friend Patrick Melroy is a pancake-ologist. He invites a gaggle of friends over every Sunday to drink coffee and eat pancakes. We love the theater of it, the waiting for our own special pancake, and the anticipation of getting a warm one right off the griddle. Equal in drama to pancakes, yet so much easier to prepare, is a Dutch baby. It's basically a luminous, eggy, and fluffy singular pancake that's related to the French clafouti and has the height and shock value of a soufflé, but it's easier to make than these delicate delights. You prepare a simple batter, then pour it into a hot buttery skillet or pan and bake. After a few minutes, boom—you have a lofty pancake with tremendous flair, ready to be cut into wedges and served with plenty of powdered sugar and lemon. I've always been in love with the popular '80s muffin flavor combo of lemons and poppy seeds, and I am happy to resurrect it in Dutch baby form—the contrasts of taste and texture are divine.

LEMON-POPPY-SEED DUTCH BABY

SERVES 4

DUTCH BABY

3 large eggs

2/3 cup whole milk

1/3 cup all-purpose flour

1/3 cup almond meal

Pinch of freshly grated nutmeg

1/2 teaspoon fine sea salt

1 tablespoon poppy seeds

1 teaspoon vanilla extract

4 tablespoons unsalted butter, cubed

TOPPING

1/3 cup powdered sugar

1 tablespoon grated lemon zest

1 teaspoon poppy seeds

Lemon wedges, for squeezing

Preheat the oven to 450°F. Put a 10-inch pie pan (glass or metal) or cast-iron skillet on a baking sheet onto the middle rack of the oven.

PREPARE THE DUTCH BABY: In a blender, combine the eggs, milk, flour, almond meal, nutmeg, salt, poppy seeds, and vanilla. Whizz on high speed for about 30 seconds, until everything is combined in a runny batter. (It will be looser than traditional American pancake batter, more similar to crepe batter.)

Remove the heated pie pan or skillet from the oven and add the butter, swirling a little, until it has melted completely and the sides and bottom are completely coated. Pour in the batter and return the pan to the oven. Bake for 18 to 20 minutes, until the pancake is puffed and golden brown.

SERVE THE DUTCH BABY: Dust with sifted powdered sugar, then top with lemon zest and 1 teaspoon poppyseeds. Invite each guest to squeeze lemon juice onto their slices.

CHOCOLATE-ORANGE CHALLAH WITH SAFFRON

MAKES ONE 10-INCH
CHALLAH BREAD

My friend Deena Prichep blogged about a version of this challah on her blog *Mostly Foodstuffs*, and I've taken it one step further along the telephone game with dark chocolate, orange zest, flaky salt, saffron, and pink sugar balls. We're deviating from the Jewish tradition of our ancestors here and landing in a disco party out west for Shabbat.

¾ cup whole milk

Large pinch of saffron threads

⅓ cup olive oil, plus more for greasing the bowl

2¼ teaspoons (1 envelope) active dry yeast

2 large eggs

2 egg yolks

⅓ cup agave syrup

1 teaspoon fine sea salt

2 teaspoons grated orange zest

4 to 4½ cups all-purpose flour

1 cup roughly chopped dark (72% cacao) chocolate (one 4-ounce bar; I like Valrhona)

Flaky sea salt, for garnish

Pink sugar balls, for garnish

In a small saucepan, bring the milk almost to a boil. Add the saffron, cover, and remove from the heat. Let the milk steep for about 1 hour. Grease a large bowl with olive oil and set aside.

In the bowl of an electric stand mixer fitted with the paddle attachment, combine the steeped milk and yeast. Allow the yeast to bloom for about 5 minutes, until it produces a creamy liquid with bubbles on top. Whisk in 1 whole egg, the egg yolks, oil, agave syrup, fine sea salt, and orange zest. Adding 1 cup at a time, mix the flour into the wet mixture until a shaggy dough has started to form. Change to the dough hook and knead the dough on low speed until the dough is a smooth, soft texture, 5 to 7 minutes (or if you're kneading by hand, work the dough for about 10 minutes). Place the dough in the greased bowl, cover with plastic wrap, and let rise until doubled in size, 1 to 2 hours.

Punch the dough down and divide into 4 equal sections. Spread each portion into a 12-inch-long rectangle about 1 inch thick, top with the chocolate shards, and roll up each rectangle into a rope.

Set 2 ropes parallel to each other on a counter and the other 2 perpendicular in direction on top, with about 1 square inch of space at the center. Starting with the piece at the top right, turn it under the rope at 3 o'clock and bring it on top of the second rope at the 3 o'clock position. Moving in a clockwise direction, pick up the next rope (you've just gone under its neighbor), and repeat the process, weaving under the rope that lies to the immediate right of the rope you're holding. When there is no more rope to work with, pinch the last piece under.

Set the woven dough on a baking sheet, cover it lightly with a tea towel, and allow it to rise for 1 hour. Preheat the oven to 375°F. In a small bowl, beat the remaining egg with 1 teaspoon water. Brush the loaf with the egg wash and sprinkle with flaky salt and sugar balls. Bake the challah for 35 to 40 minutes, until golden brown. Let cool completely on a wire rack, then slice and serve.

LEMON-LAVENDER FRENCH TOAST

SERVES 6

This baked French toast is what sparkly little fairies eat on their days off from giving gold coins to children, dancing on toadstools, and making flowers bloom. (I swear.) The marriage of lemon, lavender, brioche, and a touch of nutmeg is rich and swoonworthy. Each bite is more heady and aromatic than the last, especially with extra syrup, blueberries, and a generous blob of tangy Icelandic yogurt.

FRENCH TOAST

10 thick slices (¾ inch) brioche bread

Unsalted butter, for greasing the baking dish

1 cup whole milk

½ cup heavy (whipping) cream

1 whole vanilla bean, halved lengthwise

10 fresh whole lavender flowers, chopped, plus more sprigs for garnish

4 large eggs

½ cup sugar

½ teaspoon fine sea salt

¼ teaspoon freshly grated nutmeg

1 tablespoon grated lemon zest

1 teaspoon vanilla extract

SYRUP

½ cup maple syrup

¼ cup heavy (whipping) cream

1 tablespoon grated lemon zest

¼ cup lemon juice

Pinch of fine sea salt

Plain yogurt and fresh blueberries, for serving

MAKE THE FRENCH TOAST: Set the brioche slices out on the counter for a day to become stale (if you don't have time, you can toast them in the broiler for a minute on each side to cheat on this step). Preheat the oven to 375°F. Butter an 11 x 14-inch casserole or other ovenproof dish.

In a medium saucepan, heat the milk and cream almost to a boil, then scrape the vanilla seeds into the pot. Add the vanilla pods and chopped lavender flowers, cover, and turn off the heat. Let the milk mixture steep for 10 minutes, then strain the liquid through a fine-mesh sieve into a large bowl (discard the solids in the sieve).

In another large bowl, beat the eggs, sugar, salt, nutmeg, lemon zest, and vanilla until combined. Introduce a little egg mixture into the warm milk with a whisk, then slowly whisk the entire egg mixture into the milk, whisking constantly so nothing curdles.

Dunk each piece of brioche into the custard and arrange in a fan in the buttered dish, then pour the remaining custard onto the saturated bread. Bake for 30 minutes, or until golden brown.

MAKE THE SYRUP: Meanwhile, in a small bowl, whisk together the maple syrup, cream, lemon zest and juice, and salt.

FOR THE TOPPING: Pull the pan out of the oven and immediately pour the syrup mixture all over the French toast. Garnish with a few extra lavender flowers. Serve with the yogurt for dolloping and a bowl of blueberries.

SWEET TAHINI BUNS

MAKES 12 BUNS

I first encountered these buns years ago in Istanbul, while living there during one cold winter. We stayed on a very posh street in an apartment that was dirt cheap in the off-season. Each day I ate my way through the city, sampling treasures at every street corner café.

The tahini bun, referred to in Turkey as a "halva bun," was the most memorable treat, completely embodying Istanbul's love of sesame and perfect pastry. I became downright obsessed with it. The play of rich tahini with light crackly dough, salt with brown sugar, and savory with sweet is irresistible. This version utilizes store-bought puff pastry and can be thrown together and on the table in under 30 minutes.

1 cup tahini paste

½ teaspoon fine sea salt

½ cup packed light brown sugar

¼ cup sesame seeds

All-purpose flour, for rolling out the pastry

2 sheets frozen puff pastry (14 ounces), thawed

1 large egg

Preheat the oven to 400°F. Line a baking sheet with parchment paper.

In a large bowl, mix together the tahini paste, salt, brown sugar, and sesame seeds. Set aside.

Lightly flour a countertop and unroll the sheets of puff pastry to create one large sheet, about 10 x 20 inches and ¼-inch thick. Roll with a pin one or two times to even the dough out and unwrinkle the folds. Position the rectangle of dough horizontally so that the long sides are at the top and bottom. Spread the tahini mixture onto the pastry dough, leaving a ½-inch border at the top and bottom. Starting with the end closest to you, roll the dough tightly into a jellyroll, placing it seam-side down on a cutting board. Trim the ends (so there are no uneven buns) and cut the roll into 12 equal slices.

Place each piece spiral-side up on the prepared baking sheet. Beat the egg with 1 teaspoon water, and brush lightly over the spiral top of each bun. Bake the buns for 25 minutes, rotating the pan front to back halfway through, until they are a deep golden brown. Transfer the buns to a wire rack to cool for 2 minutes. Serve warm.

TEATIME

let's have a proper cuppa

When lunch is a distant memory and dinner seems too far off, teatime brings a sweet pick-me-up accompanied by a favorite brew. It doesn't have to be tea, though. The point is that you take a little time to reboot and relax—even a short recess from work—and punctuate the day with some midafternoon inspiration. Perhaps you're more of a coffee person, or not keen on warm beverages in the heat of the day and are craving juice, sparkling water, or lemonade. . . . The cast of characters for a modern tea party is ever-changing, depending on your preference, region of the world, and tradition.

In Sweden, this moment has a name I've always loved, *fika*, which roughly translates to coffee break but encapsulates so much more. Folks take a moment with coffee (or another drink of choice) and a sweet bread, such as a cinnamon bun, to make a purposeful redirection in the day. Try it for yourself by setting out a plate of Almond Honey Financiers (page 72) at the office; it's the quickest way to get others to join you. Or create an impromptu hang with family and friends over Matcha Egg Cream (page 57).

To take time to share tea and a snack is to affirm the good life. Amid the busyness, ceaseless deadlines, and constant hustle, pausing is a revolutionary and necessary act of kindness—to friends and also to yourself. It can take five minutes or it might drift in to a several-hour languid affair. No matter the company or the setting, equip yourself with your favorite drink in your favorite cup, a handmade bite, and a metaphorical stop sign. No one will plan this restorative, fun time for you and your pals; you've got to seize it from the day. Now stay there, zipped right in the present, and enjoy a laugh or let yourself daydream, accompanied by a crunchy, chewy Pistachio Rose Clouds (page 64), of course!

Sugar Cookies with Edible Flowers, *page 54*

SUGAR COOKIES WITH EDIBLE FLOWERS

MAKES ABOUT 3 DOZEN
2-INCH COOKIES

These flower cookies are one of the charming desserts I hold dearest. They remind me of something Lewis Carroll's Alice might encounter, long after she falls down the rabbit hole into Wonderland. Pansies, sugar, and butter are happy companions—their collective flavor sings and their beauty bewitches. I sometimes make them just for me, to add sparkle and delight to my afternoon tea ritual. When friends come over and these darlings appear, squeals and gasps abound.

COOKIES

2 tablespoons crème fraîche

2 sticks (½ pound) unsalted butter, at room temperature

1 cup powdered sugar

1 teaspoon vanilla extract

1 large egg

3 cups all-purpose flour, plus more for the work surface and rolling pin

2 teaspoons baking powder

½ teaspoon fine sea salt

1 teaspoon grated lemon zest

CANDIED FLOWERS

3 to 4 dozen organic, untreated, edible blossoms (pansies, dianthus, rose petals, calendula, chrysanthemum, lavender, cosmos, or echinacea are all good options; see Note, page 55)

1 large pasteurized egg white, lightly beaten

¼ cup turbinado sugar

PREPARE THE COOKIES: In the bowl of an electric stand mixer fitted with the paddle attachment, beat together the crème fraîche, butter, and powdered sugar until light and fluffy. Mix in the vanilla and egg until combined.

In a medium bowl, sift together the flour, baking powder, and salt. Add the flour mixture and lemon zest to the butter mixture and beat until evenly incorporated.

On a floured work surface, shape the dough into two 5-inch round disks, wrap tightly in plastic wrap or parchment, and refrigerate for at least 1 hour or up to 3 days. (Alternatively, you can freeze the disks, wrapped tightly in plastic wrap and foil, for up to 1 month. Thaw in the fridge for a day before using.)

Preheat the oven to 350°F. Line 2 baking sheets with parchment paper. Remove the dough from the refrigerator and let it rest on the counter for 5 minutes.

Dust a work surface and rolling pin with flour. Give the disks a few whacks with the rolling pin to soften them slightly. Roll out the dough to a ¼-inch thickness. Working quickly so the dough won't soften too much, use cookie cutters to punch out whatever shapes you like. Transfer the cookies to the prepared sheets, rerolling the dough scraps as you go to cut out more cookies.

Bake the cookies for 9 minutes, until the cookies are set but still pale and underdone. Transfer to a wire rack to cool slightly. Leave the oven on and set the lined baking sheets aside.

CREATE THE CANDIED FLOWERS: Set up a work station. Gather your edible flowers together. Place the egg white in a small bowl and the turbinado sugar in a second small bowl. Set out a small paintbrush. Gently dunk a flower in the egg white, taking care to get egg white in between the petals for an even pressing, then press the flower into the cookie. The delicate petals may curl up, but smooth them down with your finger. When the flower is as flat as possible, use the paintbrush to brush a thin coating of additional egg white over the entire surface of the cookie. Sprinkle with a generous pinch of the turbinado sugar. Transfer the flower-topped cookies back to the baking sheets as you work.

Return the cookies to the oven and bake for 7 to 8 minutes, until the edges of the cookies are golden. Transfer to a wire rack to cool.

note Make sure to purchase edible, untreated, organic flowers for this, or grow your own. Keep in mind, the colors of the flowers you select will darken as you bake them, giving an antique color effect.

This recipe is part nostalgia for the egg cream from my Grandma Ruthy's Brooklyn apartment and part ancient Japanese tradition. But how do all these eclectic ideas become one effervescent beverage? The bubbles, the caffeine, and the touch of sugar will positively light you on fire and deliver happy juju for the next couple of hours. I can personally attest that many pages of this very book were written while I was fueled by the buzz of this crazy concoction. And although the recipe calls for just a teensy bit of condensed milk, it's well worth the purchase (any leftover condensed milk holds up in the fridge for a long time and is delicious in morning coffee and tea).

This is an extreme departure from the traditional egg cream, a strangely titled (as it contains no egg or cream) Jewish deli staple of seltzer water, chocolate syrup, and milk. My bubbe would be confused by my version—where is the chocolate and what's with the condensed milk?—and probably shudder at the thought. But occasionally, change is good, and I like to think of some alternate universe where I could travel to Grandma's apartment on a hot afternoon, after a long day of museum hopping, and mix up a couple of matcha egg creams for us to enjoy on her balcony as the day fades.

MATCHA EGG CREAM

SERVES 2

2 cups ice

2 teaspoons matcha powder (see Note)

1/2 cup whole milk

3 tablespoons sweetened condensed milk

1¼ cups carbonated water

Place 2 large glasses full of ice into the freezer to get frosty.

In a screw-top pint jar, combine the matcha, whole milk, and condensed milk and screw on the lid securely. Vigorously shake the jar until the contents are uniformly combined. Take the glasses from the freezer and pour half of the matcha milk into each glass. Top each glass with carbonated water. Swirl with a large spoon and enjoy immediately.

note You can find matcha powder, a finely ground green tea, at fine tea and coffee shops, Asian markets, and fancy grocery stores.

VEGAN HOT CHOCOLATE WITH COCONUT CREAM

SERVES 4

When I'm desperate for a chocolate fix, I prefer a small cup of very potent, liquid dark chocolate over a large mug of the watery stuff. I like to have my mouth coated in a rich, barely sweetened concoction—from that very first sip, my endorphins skyrocket and I can't help but smile. Once I decided to substitute coconut milk for the usual dairy milk I was immediately converted—the silky smooth texture and viscous fattiness make it stunning for a drinking chocolate. This is an assertive, take-no-prisoners confection for all the chocolate lovers out there (you know who you are!).

1 can (14 ounces) whole-fat coconut milk (see Note, page 59)

1 tablespoon granulated sugar

½ cup unsweetened shredded coconut

1 cup unsweetened almond milk

¼ cup unsweetened cocoa powder, sifted

3 tablespoons dark brown sugar

1 teaspoon vanilla extract

Pinch of fine sea salt

Refrigerate the can of coconut milk for 8 hours, or overnight, so the cream will rise to the top of the can.

Carefully scrape the top half of the coconut milk (the cream) into a bowl, reserving 3 tablespoons of the cream and the remaining milky water for the chocolate. It may be very firm or it may be the consistency of a thick cream, depending on your brand of coconut milk, but either will do. With an electric mixer, whisk the coconut cream for about 3 minutes, until soft peaks form. Add the granulated sugar, whisk again for 10 seconds, and set aside in the fridge.

In a small skillet, toast the coconut shreds over medium heat until golden brown. Remove from the heat and pour the coconut onto a plate to cool.

Pour the remaining separated coconut milk, reserved 3 tablespoons coconut cream, and almond milk into a medium saucepan. Add the cocoa powder, brown sugar, vanilla, and salt. Whisk over medium heat until the sugar is dissolved and the hot chocolate is warm, about 5 minutes.

To serve, provide each guest with a small teacup, an individual pitcher filled with ½ cup of the hot chocolate, a small cup with ½ cup whipped coconut cream, and a tiny bowl of 2 tablespoons shredded coconut. Everyone can doctor their drinking chocolate as they please.

note It's important to use whole-fat (not "light") coconut milk or else the cream won't separate from the water.

RHUBARB ROSE FLOATS

SERVES 4

Let's bring the ice cream float back into vogue! Who's with me? All you need is some sticky sour/sweet rhubarb syrup, which is easy enough to make. Add good-quality vanilla ice cream and sparkling water, and you've got something pretty exceptional. But if you really want to go all the way (and, like me, you enjoy a culinary project), knock out the candied rose petals ahead of time when you have an hour to spare— they keep for about a week in a sealed container and make teatime far more interesting. I cannot help but sprinkle them atop any dessert in my midst, they're so pretty!

¾ cup granulated sugar

3 cups roughly chopped rhubarb

Pinch of salt

2 cups carbonated water

4 scoops vanilla ice cream

1 cup (or more) whipped cream

Candied Rose Petals (recipe follows)

tip
Leftover rhubarb syrup is great on yogurt, other desserts, oatmeal, and even as the sweet element in a salad dressing.

In a medium saucepan, combine 1 cup water, the granulated sugar, rhubarb, and salt and bring to a boil. Reduce the heat until it's just high enough to maintain a healthy simmer, and cook for 10 minutes, stirring occasionally. Place a fine-mesh sieve over a bowl and pour the rhubarb mixture through it, pressing the pulp against the sides of the strainer to squeeze as much syrup out as possible. Reserve the pulp for another use (as a jamlike spread) and pour the syrup into a small sealable jar. (There may be a little extra than what you need here, but keep it sealed and it will stay good in the fridge for up to 2 weeks; see Tip.)

In each of 4 cocktail glasses or wineglasses, mix 2 tablespoons of the rhubarb syrup with ½ cup of carbonated water. Scoop the ice cream into each glass and top with a heaping ¼ cup whipped cream (or more if you like). Dot the top of the whipped cream with 5 candied rose petals and serve.

CANDIED ROSE PETALS

MAKES ½ CUP

20 organic untreated rose petals

1 large pasteurized egg white, lightly beaten

½ cup superfine sugar

Line a baking sheet with parchment paper. Using a small brush, paint each rose petal with a thin layer of egg white, then dust with the superfine sugar. Carefully place the petals on the parchment and let harden at room temperature for at least 8 hours (any extras can be stored in a sealed container for up to a week).

On my wedding day, I woke up with a racing heart and an ear-to-ear smile—seriously, my face hurt from smiling so hard. Being that it was the middle of July and I'm a lightweight with alcohol, I knew countless glasses of Champagne would only land me facedown on the dance floor, possibly exposing my structurally sound underwear situation (a granny girdle does wonders for a girl!). So instead, I met the day with myriad spa waters at the ready. Amazing what some fresh fruits and herbs can do for a glass of the plain stuff, to transform something you should be drinking anyway into something you look forward to. From that crazy day onward, I always keep a large pitcher of fancy water on hand, in any one of these nine endlessly adaptable varieties, just in case my only other option is Champagne.

ASSORTED SPA WATERS

MAKES 1 LITER PER BATCH

GINGER-PEACH

1 medium peach, cut into large slices

1-inch piece of fresh ginger, cut into ¼-inch slices

PINEAPPLE-MINT

⅓ pineapple, peeled, cored, and cut into 1-inch cubes

20 fresh mint leaves (or 4 big sprigs)

BLACKBERRY-SAGE

20 fresh or frozen blackberries

8 fresh sage leaves

CUCUMBER-MINT

1 small cucumber (or ½ large), cut into ¼-inch rounds

20 fresh mint leaves (or 4 big sprigs)

BLUEBERRY-LAVENDER

½ cup fresh or frozen blueberries

12 edible lavender blossoms (or 2 large sprigs)

STRAWBERRY-BASIL

⅔ cup fresh strawberries, cut into ¼-inch slices

10 fresh basil leaves

APPLE-TARRAGON

1 medium apple, cut into ¼-inch rounds

4 sprigs fresh tarragon

RASPBERRY-LEMON

10 fresh raspberries

2 slices (¼-inch) lemon

ORANGE-ROSEMARY

1 medium orange, cut into ¼-inch rounds

2 sprigs fresh rosemary

For each batch (1 liter) of spa water, place the ingredients of choice into a 1-quart canning jar and fill to the top with room temperature water. Screw on the lid and place in the sun to steep for 1 hour. Serve over ice, with a little bit of the fruit or herbs in each glass.

PISTACHIO ROSE CLOUDS

MAKES ABOUT 12

4 egg whites

½ cup granulated sugar

1 cup powdered sugar

1 teaspoon rosewater

4 drops red food coloring

Pinch of salt

½ cup finely chopped pistachios

3 tablespoons finely chopped organic, untreated rose petals

These little pink meringues have a messy elegance to them. Their delicate rose flavor and subtle crunch from pops of crushed pistachios combine for a delectable, fun eating experience. I like my meringues with a slight chew at the center, so if you prefer yours to be crunchy all the way through, bake for 15 to 20 minutes longer than the recommended time. Either way, there's nothing quite like the melt-in-your-mouth sweetness of a good meringue. They are especially tasty when accompanied by a rich, smoky black tea: Lapsang souchong is a wonderful option—its campfire-earthiness helps cut through the extreme sweetness of the meringue.

Preheat the oven to 230°F. Line a baking sheet with parchment paper.

In the bowl of an electric stand mixer fitted with the whisk attachment, whisk the egg whites at a high speed until slightly frothy. Continue to whisk at a medium-high speed, adding the granulated sugar 1 tablespoon at a time. Then add the powdered sugar in the same fashion. Add the rosewater, food coloring, and salt and turn the mixer to high. Whisk on high until the mixture is glossy and stiff peaks are formed.

Set aside 1 tablespoon of the pistachios and 1 tablespoon of the rose petals for garnish. Fold the remaining pistachios and rose petals into the meringue.

Use 2 spoons to scoop the mixture onto the parchment—one to scoop, the other to shape the meringues—forming 1½-inch mounds. The cookies don't need much room between one another; they don't expand. Dust each meringue with a pinch of the reserved pistachios and rose petals. Bake for 1 hour and 30 minutes, or until hollow sounding when tapped. Cool on a wire rack and serve immediately.

THE BEST BLACK & WHITE COOKIES

MAKES ABOUT 4 DOZEN COOKIES

The only problem with traditional black and white cookies you find in New York delis: EVERYTHING. They're usually a sad state of stale yellow cake covered in brown food dye and plain white royal icing. I flipped the switch completely with a salty, chocolaty shortbread and a handsome half-moon frosting of white chocolate, complete with a bit of fancy flair: a light sprinkle of cacao nibs. NYC cookie power restored!

1¼ cups all-purpose flour, plus more for the work surface

⅓ cup unsweetened cocoa powder

½ teaspoon baking soda

½ teaspoon coarse sea salt (fleur de sel or Light Grey Celtic would both be great here)

1 stick (4 ounces) plus 2 tablespoons unsalted butter, at room temperature

½ cup sugar

1 teaspoon vanilla extract

4 ounces white chocolate, coarsely chopped

1 tablespoon coarsely crushed cacao nibs

In a medium bowl, whisk together the flour, cocoa powder, baking soda, and salt (if your cocoa powder is particularly lumpy, you may need to sift the mixture together). Set aside.

In the bowl of an electric stand mixer fitted with the paddle attachment, cream the butter, sugar, and vanilla until light and fluffy. Add the flour mixture to the butter mixture and beat until just incorporated (the mixture will look a little crumbly, but will gradually come together). Turn the dough out onto a clean floured work surface. Use your hands to shape the dough into two 8-inch-long logs about 1 inch in diameter. Wrap the dough logs tightly in plastic wrap or parchment and refrigerate for about 4 hours, or overnight.

Preheat the oven to 350°F. Line 2 baking sheets with parchment paper. Take the chilled dough logs from the refrigerator and cut them crosswise into ¼-inch disks. Place the disks on the baking sheets, leaving a bit of space between. Bake for about 11 minutes, or until just barely set (the cookies will set up more as they cool). Gently transfer to wire racks to cool completely.

Place the white chocolate in a small microwave-safe bowl and microwave in 10-second bursts, stirring between each, until melted with just a few bits left (or you can melt it in a double boiler). Spread one half of each cookie with a spoonful of white chocolate and place back on the wire racks. Top each frosted part of the cookie with a pinch of cacao nibs. Let the white chocolate set on the cookies, about 30 minutes in a cool kitchen (or 5 minutes in the refrigerator), before enjoying.

SALTY EVERYTHING COOKIES

MAKES ABOUT 20 COOKIES

1 cup pumpkin seeds

1 tablespoon olive oil

2½ teaspoons coarse salt, plus more for sprinkling

1 cup all-purpose flour

½ cup rye flour

½ cup quinoa flour

½ cup whole wheat flour

2 tablespoons sesame seeds

2 tablespoons poppy seeds

1½ teaspoons baking powder

1 teaspoon baking soda

2 sticks (½ pound) unsalted butter, at room temperature

¾ cup packed dark brown sugar

¾ cup granulated sugar

1 teaspoon vanilla extract

2 large eggs

8 ounces bittersweet chocolate, roughly chopped

Kim Boyce is my favorite baker and is also one of the kindest, warmest souls I've met. These cookies are adapted from a recipe she developed a few years ago; they're full of whole-grain flavor and goodness, as well as notes of salt, olive oil, and large slabs of bittersweet chocolate. They're easy to make once you've stocked a few interesting flours (quinoa, rye, and whole wheat).

Preheat the oven to 325°F. Line a baking sheet with parchment paper. In a small bowl, toss the pumpkin seeds with the olive oil and 1 teaspoon of the salt. Spread in an even layer on the prepared baking sheet and bake, stirring occasionally, for 10 to 15 minutes, until golden and toasty smelling. Transfer the seeds to a bowl. Leave the oven on.

Increase the oven temperature to 375°F. Line 2 baking sheets with parchment paper. In a large bowl, whisk together the remaining 1½ teaspoons salt, the flours, sesame seeds, poppy seeds, baking powder, and baking soda. Set aside.

In the bowl of an electric stand mixer fitted with the paddle attachment, cream the butter, brown sugar, and granulated sugar until fluffy and fully incorporated. Add the vanilla and eggs, one at time, and beat until well mixed. Slowly add the flour mixture to the butter mixture and beat until just combined. Fold in half of the chocolate and half of the toasted pumpkin seeds.

Scoop out the dough in ¼-cup lumps and place on the prepared baking sheets, leaving a couple of inches between the cookies. Flatten slightly with the palm of your hand and sprinkle the remaining chocolate, pumpkin seeds, and an extra sprinkling of salt on top of the dough, pushing into the dough with the tips of your fingers.

Bake the cookies for 12 to 15 minutes, rotating the pans front to back halfway through the cooking time, until they begin to brown on the edges. Let the cookies cool for 5 minutes on the baking sheets, then transfer to a wire rack to finish cooling.

APRICOT, HAZELNUT & GINGER CANTUCCINI

MAKES ABOUT 5 DOZEN COOKIES

Every culture seems to have a brittle, crunchy cookie that's perfect for dunking into tea or morning coffee. (My grandmother used to make mandelbrot, the Jewish version studded with nuts or chocolate chips.) This recipe creates the ideal treat for washing down a dainty glass of the Tuscan fortified wine, Vin Santo, and reminds me of the rolling hills in the countryside outside of Florence. (I cook to connect with others, but also to selfishly time travel.) I learned how to make these cookies in the cozy kitchen of Giulia Scarpaleggia, a worldly Italian girl, who generously shared all her culinary secrets. These *cantuccini* are a cousin of biscotti, only with a little more chew and bursting with flavor thanks to the caramel-like apricots, toasty hazelnuts, bittersweet cacao nibs, and subtle zip of ginger.

2 large eggs, separated

2/3 cup sugar

1 tablespoon honey

1 teaspoon vanilla extract

1¾ cups all-purpose flour

½ teaspoon baking powder

½ teaspoon fine sea salt

¾ cup dried apricots, cut into ¼-inch slivers

1 cup roughly chopped hazelnuts

⅓ cup roughly chopped cacao nibs

2 tablespoons finely chopped candied ginger

Preheat the oven to 350°F. Line 2 baking sheets with parchment paper.

In the bowl of an electric stand mixer fitted with the whisk attachment, whisk the egg whites on a low speed until foamy. Gradually add the sugar and whisk, increasing the speed to high, until soft peaks are formed, about 5 minutes. In a separate small bowl, whisk together the egg yolks, honey, and vanilla. Gently fold the yolk mixture into the beaten egg whites with a spatula until evenly incorporated.

In a medium bowl, sift together the flour, baking powder, and salt. Add the flour mixture to the egg mixture all at once, stirring until just combined. Fold in the apricots, hazelnuts, cacao nibs, and ginger.

Scoop out one-quarter of the dough and place it on one of the prepared baking sheets. Smooth the dough into a blunt-edged oval about 9 inches long and 2 inches wide (if it sticks, you can moisten your hands to help smooth out the surface). Repeat with each remaining quarter of dough, until you have 4 long logs, 2 per baking sheet.

Bake the logs for 20 minutes, or until they are slightly golden on the outside. Remove from the oven, but leave the oven on. Transfer the parchment and logs to a wire rack to cool until they are slightly firm and are no longer too hot to handle.

Transfer the dough logs to a cutting board and use a serrated knife to cut them crosswise into ½-inch-thick slices, about 15 slices per log. Return the parchment to the baking sheets and place the cookies cut side up on the baking sheets. Return them to the oven and bake for about 15 minutes, flipping the cookies over halfway through. Let the cookies cool completely on the pans.

I have a secret. . . . The *financier*, an exquisitely sophisticated little almond cake, is really easy to make. These small tea cakes deserve the spotlight. Often they get lost in a tray of petits fours, scones, and other elaborate cookies, but with their toasty almond flavor and bright honey sweetness, they're the first treat I reach for. In this version, I've added a jammy blackberry to one end, which you can replace with another bit of seasonal fruit (thinly sliced pear is also divine) or, in a more traditional fashion, leave out all together and just go pure almond.

In another deviation from tradition, I've added a little quinoa flour and puffed quinoa as garnish—the slightly bitter notes help tone down the sweetness. The financier typically comes in various shapes and sizes, from flat bars to mini muffins, and they're delicious no matter their iteration. I like the 3-inch barquette mold for the dramatic oblong shape and pointy ends.

ALMOND HONEY FINANCIERS

MAKES ABOUT 12 CAKES

1 cup almond meal

2 tablespoons quinoa flour

1 tablespoon all-purpose flour, plus a little more for the tins

½ teaspoon fine sea salt

6 tablespoons unsalted butter, plus a little more for greasing the tins

⅓ cup honey

⅓ cup sugar

1 teaspoon vanilla extract

2 large eggs

12 blackberries (fresh or frozen)

¼ cup puffed quinoa, for garnish (optional)

1 tablespoon white chia seeds, for garnish (optional)

Preheat the oven to 350°F. Grease and flour 12 barquette tins (or whatever molds you're using).

In the bowl of an electric stand mixer fitted with the paddle attachment, combine the almond meal, quinoa flour, all-purpose flour, and salt.

In a small saucepan, combine the butter, honey, sugar, and vanilla and stir over medium heat until the butter is melted and the sugar is dissolved.

With the mixer on, slowly add the butter/honey mixture to the almond/flour mixture. Add the eggs, one at a time, and mix until just combined.

Place the molds on a baking sheet. Fill the molds three-quarters full with batter. Gingerly top one end with a blackberry. If desired, scatter a pinch of puffed quinoa and white chia seeds at the other end.

Bake for about 15 minutes, or until golden brown on top (see Note). Let cool in the molds for 5 minutes, then remove from the molds and let cool on a wire rack.

note Adjust baking times if using slightly smaller molds such as muffin tins; look for a deep golden color and toasty almond smell.

RAW VEGAN CACAO & COCONUT HEARTS

MAKES ABOUT 12

These healthful heart-shaped cacao treats are a DIY hack for Lärabars, a natural energy bar made mostly of dates and nuts. They are inexpensive to make, the ingredients are easy to keep on hand, and they add a touch of whimsy (and energy) to an afternoon break. Best of all, they bring cheer to anyone you gift them to: your workout buddy, your vegan friend, your gluten-free colleague, or even the neighbor's kids who just want something unfussy and sweet.

1 cup cashews

1 cup flaked coconut (best if in large flakes)

6 tablespoons raw cacao powder, plus more for dusting

¼ teaspoon fine sea salt

8 Medjool dates, pitted

In a food processor, combine all the ingredients with 3 tablespoons water and pulse until a thick dough is formed, about 2 minutes.

Press the dough into a ¾-inch-thick block on a sheet of parchment. Cut out with 2-inch heart-shaped cookie cutters (or simply into squares). Gather the scraps of dough together to cut out a few more hearts. Dust with more cacao powder and enjoy. (Store any leftovers in a covered container in the refrigerator for up to 1 week. They're good right out of the fridge or at room temperature.)

ORANGE BLOSSOM HAGELSLAG ON TOAST

SERVES 6 TO 8 (MAKES ABOUT 2 CUPS SPRINKLES)

Did you know people in Holland, young and old, put sprinkles all over buttered toast to eat for breakfast or as a snack? This is perfectly normal—no one thinks anything of a businessman with a briefcase in one hand and a festive toast in the other. The phenomenon is so widespread, there are actually entire grocery aisles dedicated to sprinkle varieties!

When I tasted the toasts, known as *hagelslag* (which means "hailstorm" in Dutch), I nearly died of happiness and the sugar-spiked high that followed. Upon returning home, I decided to ramp up my own take with homemade orange blossom–flavored sprinkles (a fun and fairly simple project, especially for kids). The cascade of sugar shards descends across the toast in an ombré pattern—so outrageous and pretty, they're almost too intense to eat. (Almost.) These toasts are the very embodiment of all my bejeweled fairy-tale princess and tea party fantasies; one bite and they're guaranteed to make you sprout fairy wings.

3 cups powdered sugar

½ teaspoon salt

2 large egg whites (see Note, page 157)

1 teaspoon orange blossom water

10 drops red or pink food coloring

8 slices white bread

4 tablespoons unsalted butter, at room temperature

Line 4 baking sheets with parchment paper.

In a large bowl, whisk together the powdered sugar, salt, egg whites, and orange blossom water. Whisk vigorously until it has a smooth, viscous consistency.

Scoop out one-third of the mixture into a zip-seal plastic bag. Use the food coloring to tint the remaining sugar mixture in the bowl a light, barely pink color. Scoop out another one-third of that mixture into a second plastic bag. Tint the remaining sugar mixture with another few drops of food coloring for a darker color and transfer half of that to a third plastic bag. Add a few more drops of food coloring to create a rich color for the remaining mixture.

Take one of the plastic bags of sugar mixture and snip the tip off, leaving a small opening. Pipe long, thin stripes of icing onto the parchment, until you've used up the mixture. Repeat with the remaining bags and baking sheets. Keep colors separate to achieve an ombré effect. Let sit overnight, or up to 24 hours, until totally dry.

When the lines of icing are dry, turn them into sprinkles! Using a bench scraper or metal spatula, scrape along the edges of the icing lines to remove from the parchment. (It will break up into sprinkle-size bits as you do this, but if they're not small enough, run your scraper or a knife through them to chop them even more finely.) Keep each color separate until ready to decorate.

Toast the bread to your preferred level of crispiness. Slather each piece of toast with a generous dollop of softened butter. Sprinkle the sprinkles in an ombré pattern, from richest color to lightest, covering the entire toast. Serve immediately.

SOUTH INDIAN KESARI BHATH WITH TOASTED CASHEWS, SULTANAS & SAFFRON

SERVES 6 TO 8

Kesari bhath, one of South India's most beloved snack foods, sounds exotic, but it's easy to make and enjoy. There are many variations of this delicate mound of gently spiced whole wheat farina, but my husband and I discovered our favorite during a breakfast at a spectacular, colorful wedding, served on banana leaves at a village temple in Belur, Karnataka. We were invited to this grand occasion moments before and rearranged our sightseeing plans to accommodate the generous offer—the wedding was a "simple country affair" (the uncle of the bride's words) and included about 500 guests! Making a batch of this sweet kesari bhath warms my soul with its heavenly floral notes, toasted wheat, jewel-like plumped raisins, and the memory of a magical day where we were welcomed into a family's special moment.

KESARI BHATH

3 tablespoons ghee or coconut oil, plus a little extra for greasing the teacups

1 cup Cream of Wheat

1 cup mango nectar

1/3 cup sugar

1/2 teaspoon fine sea salt

1 teaspoon vanilla extract

1/2 teaspoon saffron

1/2 teaspoon ground cardamom

1/4 teaspoon ground ginger

1/3 cup golden raisins

1/3 cup cut-up dried mango (1/2-inch-wide pieces)

TOPPING

1 tablespoon ghee or coconut oil

1/2 cup cashews

1/3 cup ground pistachios, for garnish (optional)

START KESARI BHATH: In a large skillet, melt the ghee over medium heat. Add the Cream of Wheat and toast, until golden in color and a toasty aroma is present, about 5 minutes. Set aside.

In a medium saucepan, combine the mango nectar, 1 cup water, the sugar, salt, vanilla, saffron, cardamom, and ginger and bring to a boil. Remove from the heat, add the raisins and mango, cover, and let sit for about 5 minutes.

MAKE THE TOPPING: In a small skillet, combine the 1 tablespoon ghee and the cashews and cook over high heat, stirring constantly, until the cashews are golden and aromatic, 3 to 5 minutes. Set aside.

Stir the toasted Cream of Wheat into the juice mixture. Return the pan to medium heat and cook for about 4 minutes, until it thickens.

Lightly grease teacups or small ramekins with a little ghee or coconut oil. Working quickly, place about 3/4 cup of the porridge into each teacup, pressing gently into the form. Serve immediately with toasted cashews and ground pistachios.

HAPPY HOUR

because it's 5 o'clock somewhere

When the sun begins to fade into the golden hour of twilight, it's time
to tuck the day's work out of sight, and switch on the record player.
I love the sound of ice cubes clinking in a glass and languid sighs
perfuming the air while a cocktail is gently poured and a few snacks are
set out. Whether just for you or many friends, the art of hanging out
takes a tiny bit of forethought; most of the recipes in this chapter can
be made in the morning and sit in the fridge or at room temperature
until you're ready for them—perfect for a last-minute hang when the
day takes a small pause before dinnertime.

Cocktail hour is perhaps the best way to travel time and distance
through little nibbles from around the world. Nowhere is this limbo
space more revered than in Argentina, where the leisurely hours before
late-night dinners can be the culinary highlight of the day—such as
Chard Empanadas with Pistachio Crema (page 106) served with a crisp,
juicy wine. If you're in the mood to blow minds with visual splendor,
turn to the Beet-Pickled Eggs (page 92) inspired by a mellow bar in
Portland and my ancestors in Eastern Europe. A light, five-minute-to-
assemble option that pairs well with a gin and tonic any time of year is
a plate of Cotija, Apricot & Rosemary Crisps (page 105), which utilize
pantry staples and the broil setting on any oven. No matter how busy
you are or how insane the day was, a small nibble with some bubbly can
alter your mood for the better and make life feel just as effervescent.

MANGO SORBET ROSÉ SPARKLER

SERVES 4

1 pint mango sorbet

1 cup sparkling rosé

12 green grapes, chilled and halved

8 Apricot, Hazelnut & Ginger Cantuccini (page 70; optional)

Did you know that Jayne Mansfield bathed in pink Champagne in her heart-shaped tub? Needless to say, once I found that out I've been obsessed with blushing bubbles ever since. Like Jayne, I always have a good bottle stashed in the fridge, because nothing says celebration like a little bubbly, and nothing starts off a lovely celebration like sparkling rosé! This cocktail is hardly a recipe, just a suggestion and a great one at that. Douse the mango sorbet with a few splashes of bubbly and stick some ice-cold grapes in a pretty glass. And there you have it: a delightful treat, perfect for the most glam of Oscar parties, casual outdoor picnics (just bring everything in a cooler and watch the eyes light up), or, if you're like me, an old-timey movie night curled up on the couch with your glamorous mom.

Place 1 scoop of sorbet in each of 4 pretty glasses. Top the sorbet with ¼ cup sparkling rosé and then 5 to 6 grape halves. Serve immediately with a few cantuccini or other simple cookies on the side, if desired.

note Smoked black sesame seeds, available at Asian groceries or Whole Foods, add an edge of flavor that cannot be replaced.

TARTINES & SMALL TOASTS

A *tartine* is a French open-faced sandwich—especially one that includes a rich spread. There is nothing more satisfying and easy to make than a crusty, toasty nibble topped with loads of flavorful ingredients. These make the perfect appetizer, cocktail bite, and midnight snack just before climbing into bed (they're actually delicious to eat in bed, too!). And once you become accustomed to stocking the larder and fridge with a small range of organic produce and artisan goods (page 8), you'll find so much potential in a lingering loaf of bread and a few choice toppings. Let little toasts rejoice!

BEET-TINTED CHÈVRE & RADISH TOASTS

SERVES 4

4 slices German-style hearty brown bread

4 ounces goat cheese

⅓ cup shredded (¼-inch pieces) raw beet (about 1 small)

1 tablespoon fresh lemon juice

½ garlic clove, finely minced

4 radishes, sliced as thin as possible

Smoked black sesame seeds, for garnish (see Note, page 84)

Chopped fresh chives, for garnish

I've been throwing pink parties since I was a kid—the menu always included some beet concoction, salmon, a mountain of pink Snoballs (they were all looks and no taste, but wow, what an impact!), pink crowns, a piñata, and a present to play "pass-the-parcel" with. . . . These beet-tinted tartines will be my pièce de résistance at my next pink party, to be sure. They tickle the palate with the garlicky creamy goat cheese (with a flavor that's a tad reminiscent of ranch dressing. That's right, I said it—ranch dressing is divine!) and the sharp spice of a farmers' market radish. Above all, they delight the eyes with pink power—all party eaters will go nuts.

Toast the bread slices well. Set aside.

In a food processor, pulse the goat cheese, beet, lemon juice, and garlic several times until you have a semismooth uniform pink mixture, about 1 minute. Spread a heaping tablespoon on each toast (you'll have a little left over, but it's delicious for swirling into scrambled eggs or atop pasta).

Top the cheese mixture with the thin radish slices, creating a pattern if you like, or random polka dots—both ways are beautiful. Sprinkle a tiny bit of black sesame seeds at the center of each radish (or add with abandon). Finish with the chives in a similar fashion and serve.

CHARRED LEMONY ASPARAGUS & RACLETTE

SERVES 2

2 large slices crusty sourdough bread

2 tablespoons olive oil

1 garlic clove, halved

1 teaspoon Dijon mustard

½ pound asparagus, ends trimmed

½ teaspoon grated lemon zest, plus a little extra for garnish

Juice of ½ lemon

Fine sea salt and freshly ground black pepper

½ cup thinly sliced Raclette cheese

Red pepper flakes, for garnish

Asparagus are the harbingers of springtime and make a great toast topper, their nuttiness highlighted by plucky lemon and the subtle sweetness of a Raclette. The magic of hot bubbling cheese, zippy lemon vinaigrette, and a hearty vegetable is not to be missed. Often, vegetarian sandwiches get relegated to the unimaginative, overly virtuous realm of sprouts and dry bread. This toasty little number swings in the complete opposite direction and gets everyone going—meat eaters and veggie-sauruses unite under these satisfying flavors.

Preheat the broiler. Place the bread on a baking sheet and drizzle each slice with 1 teaspoon of the olive oil. Broil for 4 minutes, flipping the bread halfway through, until both sides are a nice golden brown. Remove from the oven and rub one side with the halved garlic clove. Finely crush the remaining garlic clove half through a press and set aside for the dressing. Spread the toasts with the mustard. Set aside on the baking sheet. Leave the broiler on.

Meanwhile, in a medium cast-iron skillet, heat 1 teaspoon of the olive oil over high heat. Add the asparagus and cook, undisturbed, for about 2 minutes (there may be a little smoke). Flip the asparagus and cook until portions have a bit of blackening, about 3 minutes longer. Remove from the heat.

In a small bowl, whisk together the remaining olive oil, lemon zest, lemon juice, and reserved crushed garlic. Season with salt and pepper to taste. Toss the charred asparagus in the dressing.

Arrange the asparagus spears on the toasts, top with the Raclette slices, and broil for 1 to 2 minutes, until the cheese is melted. Top with a light sprinkle of pepper flakes and a little more lemon zest and serve immediately.

TOSTADA DE TOMATE

SERVES 4

4 garlic cloves, peeled

1 cup olive oil

4 Roma (plum) tomatoes

4 ciabatta rolls, split

Fine sea salt and freshly ground black pepper

⅓ cup micro greens (optional garnish)

This was my brother's breakfast at his neighborhood café in Granada, Spain. Each region in Spain does their "tomato toast" slightly differently, but this version is my favorite by far. Like a lot of Spanish food, it's simple and completely dependent on top-quality ingredients. Serve this as a light bite with a cold beer in the summertime or as a great breakfast when paired with a café con leche. I love it because this is a dish that can be made with what I typically have on hand at home: a tomato lingering in my kitchen, some day-old bread revived with a bit of toasting, good olive oil, and garlic. All these things make for a truly delicious nibble.

Lightly bruise the garlic cloves by giving them a whack with the back of a knife, then place in a jar with the olive oil and seal. Set aside at room temperature for at least 24 hours, to infuse the oil with the garlic flavor. When ready to use, strain out the garlic. (Garlic oil will keep for a few days in the refrigerator; you can use the leftover garlic cloves in a salad dressing or as a base for a tomato sauce.)

Shred each tomato, skin and all, on the large holes of a box grater (like you'd use for shredding cheddar) into a bowl.

Preheat the broiler. Arrange the split ciabatta rolls on a baking sheet and broil for 2 or 3 minutes, until just toasted.

To serve, dollop each toast half with a heaping tablespoon of shredded tomato. Spoon 1 tablespoon of the garlic oil over the tomato. Serve with the remaining olive oil on the side (guests may want a little more oil) and plenty of salt and pepper. Garnish with a large pinch of micro greens, if desired.

THE QUEEN BEE

SERVES 4

2 tablespoons raw wheat germ

2 teaspoons bee pollen

2 tablespoons unsalted butter

4 slices brown bread, such as
multigrain, toasted well

2 teaspoons honey

Maldon salt

I have a feeling that when nibbling at a cocktail hour these days, as everyone is mingling with cheeses, olives, and charcuterie, it's a radical choice to have a piece of toast. I've never gotten over the feel of my teeth crunching down on a warmed, buttered piece of bread, and I enjoy it on a regular basis.

For those who love such an indulgence, this version of toast—which resembles the night sky, with systems, darkness, stars, and planetary shards of flaky salt—is otherworldly. The combined texture of wheat germ (a gluten-free nightmare, I know, with wheat on wheat), silky pollen, sweet honey, butter, and a touch of salt becomes a warm eclectic topping, reminiscent of a nut butter without any nuts being present—full of delicate floral notes and a savory unctuous crunch. This unusual item pairs great with a Greyhound or Gin Swizzle, the sweet/savory complementing the citrus in a lovely way.

Preheat the oven to 400°F. Line a baking sheet with parchment paper.

Spread the wheat germ on the parchment in an even layer. Bake for about 4 minutes, until the wheat germ becomes fragrant. Remove from the oven and set aside.

Place the bee pollen in a mortar and pound with a pestle to turn it into a fine powder.

Spread ½ tablespoon butter on each piece of toast. Drizzle ½ teaspoon honey on top. Dust 1 teaspoon toasted wheat germ on each toast (you will have a little extra left over, but it's delicious on yogurt or in a smoothie). Dust ½ teaspoon of the ground bee pollen on each toast. Finally, sprinkle a pinch of Maldon salt (or any other good-quality flake salt you enjoy) on top. Serve immediately.

SPICE-ROASTED CHICKPEAS

SERVES 4

1 can (15 ounces) chickpeas, drained and rinsed

3 tablespoons olive oil

1 teaspoon smoked paprika

Fine sea salt

2 teaspoons fennel seeds

2 garlic cloves still in their skins, smashed with the flat side of a knife

Grated zest of ½ lemon

1 handful of fresh parsley, minced

My favorite legume just got an upgrade with a heavy dusting of Iberian spices like paprika, garlic, and a glug of good olive oil—all ingredients commonly found in Spanish cuisine and so good with chickpeas. This snack will keep you going with a nutritious dose of protein and will be a welcome addition to any appetizer platter—a nice, plant-based nibble to balance out all that cheese and charcuterie. Best of all, they have a satisfying, audible crunch when you pop them in your mouth!

Preheat the oven to 400°F.

In a medium bowl, toss the chickpeas with the olive oil, smoked paprika, ½ teaspoon salt, the fennel seeds, and garlic cloves. Spread in a single layer on a rimmed baking sheet. Roast the chickpeas until they are golden brown and crunchy, about 45 minutes, stirring once or twice during cooking.

Remove and let cool for 10 minutes. Toss with the lemon zest and parsley. Season with more salt, if desired, and serve.

note You can prepare the dish in advance, and it actually tastes better after a few hours in the fridge— perfect for when you want to have a few friends over for a bite, and don't want to be in the kitchen the whole time.

Spice-Roasted Chickpeas, *page 89*

BLOOD ORANGE & FETA STACKS

SERVES 4

These stacks are inspired by a winter farmers' market haul—when we need brightness and cheer more than ever. The sweet, juicy orange slices playfully interact with the bracing red onions, the crunchy carrots, the salty feta, and the verdant mint, all topped with the subtle heat of pepper flakes. It's a real play of textures and flavors, all coming together in a semicrazed harmony.

3 tablespoons olive oil

3 tablespoons white wine vinegar

Sea salt and freshly ground black pepper

4 medium blood oranges

¾ cup finely crumbled feta cheese

1 medium carrot, peeled into ribbons

¼ red onion, sliced into half moons as thinly as possible

Leaves from 1 bunch fresh mint

Red pepper flakes

In a small bowl, whisk together the olive oil and vinegar. Add salt and pepper to taste.

Peel the oranges and cut them crosswise into ¼-inch-thick rounds. In a wide dish, assemble each stack starting with 1 orange slice, a thin layer of feta, 1 carrot ribbon, a few slices of onion, and 1 teaspoon salad dressing. Repeat the layers 3 more times. Make a total of 4 stacks in this fashion and top each with any extra onion. Set the dish in the fridge for about 1 hour to allow the flavors to meld.

When ready to serve, scatter the mint leaves all over the serving plates. Put a stack in the center of each plate and scatter with more mint. Dust with a generous pinch of pepper flakes. Top with a little more salad dressing and season with salt and black pepper to taste.

BEET-PICKLED EGGS

SERVES 4 TO 6

As a kid, I feared the party platter of deviled eggs—too much mayonnaise, a rubbery white texture, and no tang to balance all the flavors! But a few years ago, I sat down at the bar of Grüner, a superhip little place in Portland, and after enjoying a plate of beet-pickled eggs, my tune changed. I came to learn that beet pickling is a *thang* amid Pennsylvania Dutch and folks all over Northern Europe—maybe even my people, Eastern European Jews, made such wondrous jewel-toned edibles. These eggs will steal the show at any party—they're almost too pretty to eat. The eggs are slightly sweet, salty, and have the sour spice I crave—they're the way deviled eggs should be, with a little personality, bright color, and panache.

PICKLED EGGS

8 large eggs

⅓ cup packed light brown sugar

½ cup white wine vinegar

1 teaspoon sea salt

1 teaspoon cumin seeds

1 teaspoon yellow mustard seeds

1 teaspoon fennel seeds

2 garlic cloves, halved lengthwise

4 small boiled and peeled beets (reserve cooking water) or 1 can (15 ounces) beets

FILLING

1 teaspoon dry mustard

3 tablespoons plain whole-milk yogurt

1 tablespoon mayonnaise

½ teaspoon turmeric

½ teaspoon ground cumin

1 tablespoon finely chopped fresh chives

1 tablespoon lemon juice

Fine sea salt and freshly ground black pepper

GARNISH

2 sprigs fresh marjoram

Water-packed capers

1 tablespoon minced red onion

START THE EGGS: Place the eggs in a pot and add cold water to cover by 1 or 2 inches. Bring to a boil, uncovered, then remove the pot from the heat and immediately cover with a lid. Allow the eggs to sit for 12 minutes. Plunge the boiled eggs into a bowl of ice water. When they are cool, peel the eggs (see Note, page 93) and set aside.

In a 32-ounce jar, mix together 1 cup water, the brown sugar, vinegar, salt, cumin seeds, mustard seeds, fennel seeds, and garlic. Add the beets and ½ cup of the beet water and stir to combine. Put the peeled eggs in the beet brine and refrigerate for about 24 hours (or up to 3 days for very pickled, pink eggs).

MAKE THE FILLING: Cut the brined eggs in half lengthwise and scoop the egg yolks into a medium bowl. Add the dry mustard, yogurt, mayonnaise, turmeric, ground cumin, chives, and lemon juice and mix with a fork, smashing everything together. Season with salt and pepper to taste.

GARNISH THE EGGS: Scoop a heaping teaspoon of filling into each hard-boiled egg half. Add 1 or 2 marjoram leaves, capers, and a pinch of red onion. Finish with a little salt and pepper and serve immediately.

note Try to find the oldest eggs at the grocery in order to cleanly peel the egg shell from the white of the egg; even 10 days can make a difference in how the shell comes off—sounds weird, but it works!

note I love to use *color*—and this beauty is as jewel-toned as they come—as a springboard for thinking of new recipes and flavor combinations.

PURPLE CAULIFLOWER HUMMUS

SERVES 6 TO 8

1 whole head garlic

5 tablespoons olive oil

1 purple cauliflower (about 1¼ pounds), cut into florets

Fine sea salt

3 tablespoons lemon juice

Freshly ground black pepper

Lemon wedges, for serving

Many of you know hummus in its traditional chickpea form, and of that version I am a big fan. However, when life gives you the chance to turn a popular sand-colored dip into something that looks like a Monet water lily, you just get on board the Technicolor bus and you never go back! Your crudités platter of assorted vegetables and crackers will never look the same with this colorful addition. Purple cauliflower is available in the cooler months of the year at most farmers' markets, and I see it cropping up at many organic groceries now, too.

Position a rack in the middle of the oven and preheat to 400°F. Line a baking sheet with parchment paper.

Peel off most of the papery outer layer from the head of garlic, but leave the head intact. Cut across the very top of the head to expose the cloves. Place the garlic on a sheet of foil and drizzle with 1 tablespoon olive oil. Crumple the edges of the foil around the garlic to make a packet for roasting and set aside.

In a medium bowl, combine the cauliflower, ½ teaspoon salt, and 2 tablespoons of the olive oil and toss until the cauliflower is well coated. Spread the cauliflower on the lined baking sheet without overcrowding, and nestle the garlic packet next to the cauliflower. Roast the vegetables on the middle rack for about 40 minutes—the garlic may take about 10 minutes longer than the cauliflower to roast, so check its doneness (it should be soft and spreadable) when you take the cauliflower out of the oven.

Transfer the roasted cauliflower to a food processor. Add the remaining 2 tablespoons olive oil, the lemon juice, and pepper to taste. Squeeze the roasted garlic out of its skins into the processor, then pulse until completely smooth and spreadable, 3 to 4 minutes. (If it is still chunky after a few minutes of blending, try adding a tablespoon or two of water.)

Serve with plenty of extra lemon wedges (the lemon juice will turn the purple mixture hot pink), salt, and pepper.

How can I say this without a pun? Not possible! This corn is just so *corny*. It's bursting with spice, coconut flavor, tangy lime, and a light touch of heat. There's nothing better to celebrate the arrival of summer than a little cup of this sassy snack and a gin and tonic. I like to serve this in small Weck jars with about ½ cup of the corn in each portion, with a few extra lime wedges and chili powder on top. I first had a version of this while walking the main drag in Panaji, Goa. It was the kickoff to Diwali, the festival of lights, and the week of celebrations featuring float making, firecrackers, and parades was just getting underway. Several street food stalls served a variety of intense foods to hungry onlookers, but this spiced corn was the highlight of the evening! Here's my take on it, which uses coconut oil in place of ghee and a lot of fragrant lime.

MASALA CORN

SERVES 6 TO 8

1 tablespoon coconut oil

½ of a serrano pepper, thinly sliced

1 teaspoon cumin seeds

½ teaspoon mustard seeds

½ teaspoon chili powder, plus more for garnish (optional)

Kernels from 4 ears of corn (about 3 cups)

Juice of 1 lime

2 garlic cloves, minced

3 scallions, thinly sliced

½ cup roughly chopped cilantro, plus more for garnish

Fine sea salt and freshly ground black pepper

Lime wedges, for serving

In a large skillet, melt the coconut oil over medium heat. Once the oil is hot, add the serrano pepper, cumin seeds, mustard seeds, and chili powder. Stir the spices until they are aromatic and the mustard seeds are popping (watch out for the popping hot oil!).

Add the corn and lime juice and cook, stirring constantly, until the corn just starts to become transparent and the rawness has cooked away, about 3 minutes. Remove from the heat and stir in the garlic, scallions, and the ½ cup of cilantro. Season with salt and pepper to taste.

To serve, divide the corn among cups and top each with a little cilantro, a lime wedge, and a pinch of chili powder, if desired.

SOUTH INDIAN-STYLE VEG CUTLETS

MAKES TEN 2-INCH CUTLETS

These veg cutlets are a pretty close approximation of one of my favorite dishes from Southern India, served at all the little roadside cafés and coffee shops, a true Indian fast food. The cutlets are good hot off the pan and are also tasty hours later. What I like about them is that they have a kind of mellow flavor, and when you're in India (or at home) eating all kinds of strong flavors all day long, it's nice to have a little break and eat something cozy and slightly familiar. These are often served with ketchup, but I think the Spiced Mango Butter (page 198) is really something else—it elevates the whole dish into a pretty perfect finger food.

3 small russet (baking) potatoes (about 1¼ pounds), peeled and chopped into 1-inch pieces

¾ cup diced green beans

¾ cup diced carrots

¼ cup roughly chopped salted roasted cashews

1 tablespoon coconut oil, plus more for frying

1 tablespoon minced fresh ginger

2 garlic cloves, minced

1 shallot, minced

1 teaspoon mustard seeds

1 teaspoon cumin seeds

½ teaspoon ground turmeric

½ teaspoon chili powder

¼ teaspoon ground cinnamon

½ teaspoon fine sea salt

½ cup all-purpose flour

1 cup fine dried breadcrumbs

Fresh cilantro leaves, for garnish

Set up a big bowl of ice and water. In a medium pot, combine the potatoes with water to cover generously. Bring to a boil and cook the potatoes until almost cooked through, about 15 minutes (poke with a fork and they should still be slightly firm). Add the green beans and carrots and cook for 5 minutes. Drain the vegetables and immediately place in the ice water bath to stop their cooking. Leave the vegetables in the ice bath for about 2 minutes, then drain the vegetables once more. Transfer the vegetables to a bowl and add the cashews. Using your hands or a fork, crush the potatoes until only a few large chunks remain.

In a large skillet, melt the 1 tablespoon coconut oil over medium-high heat. Add the ginger, garlic, shallot, the spices, and salt and cook until fragrant, about 2 minutes. Stir in the potato mixture and cook until all the spices are evenly incorporated and any residual moisture has cooked out, 2 to 3 minutes longer. Spoon the mixture into a bowl.

Once the mixture has cooled slightly, use your hands to form 2-inch-wide cutlets about ½ inch thick (the shape is similar to a small veggie burger). Set them on a plate as you work (you'll have about 10 patties total).

In a shallow dish, whisk together the flour and 1 cup water. Spread the breadcrumbs in a separate dish. Carefully dredge each cutlet gingerly in the flour batter, then in the breadcrumbs, handling each one delicately so it doesn't fall apart. Place the breaded cutlets on a plate until ready to fry.

In a large nonstick skillet, melt about ¼ inch of coconut oil over medium heat. Place as many cutlets in the pan as you can comfortably flip without overcrowding. Cook the cutlets until golden brown on both sides, flipping once, about 15 minutes total. Transfer the finished cutlets to a plate lined with paper towels to soak up any remaining grease. Let cool for at least 5 minutes before serving, to help the cutlets firm up. Garnish with cilantro leaves.

SOCCA CAKES WITH LABNEH & FENNEL

SERVES 6 TO 8

¾ cup labneh or ½ (1-pound) container

½ cup plus 2 tablespoons olive oil

1 large egg

1 dried fig, finely chopped

1 teaspoon finely chopped fresh rosemary

Fine sea salt

1 cup chickpea flour

2 fennel bulbs, trimmed (fronds reserved for garnish) and cut into ¼-inch-thick slices

2 teaspoons grated lemon zest

2 tablespoons lemon juice

Freshly ground black pepper

Coconut oil, for frying the cakes

Socca goes by many names in many cultures, but the essential ingredients are all the same: chickpea flour, water, and oil baked or fried up into a pancake. I've had versions of this nutty, satisfying snack in the Liguria region of Italy, in Provence in Southern France, and in the Gujarat state in Western India. A little slice or an individual cake is just the thing to accompany a glass of chilled rosé wine after a long day. This iteration takes things one step further, topping the unctuous cake with a lovely dab of labneh, my favorite Middle Eastern tangy cheese, and braised fennel.

In a large bowl, whisk together ¼ cup of the labneh, ½ cup of the olive oil, the egg, fig, rosemary, and ½ teaspoon salt until combined. Add 1 cup lukewarm water and the chickpea flour and whisk until a batter is formed. Set aside to rest for 15 minutes.

Meanwhile, in a medium skillet, heat the remaining 2 tablespoons olive oil over medium heat. Add the fennel and cook for about 2 minutes, until it starts to soften. Stir in the lemon zest, lemon juice, and a pinch each of salt and pepper and cook, stirring constantly, until softened, about 2 minutes longer. Remove the pan from the heat and set the fennel aside.

Preheat the oven to 200°F. Line a baking sheet with parchment paper.

In a large nonstick pan, melt a thin, even layer of coconut oil over medium heat. Working in batches, spoon 2 tablespoons of socca batter onto the pan for each pancake and let cook, undisturbed, until bubbles emerge on the surface, about 3 minutes. Flip the pancakes and let the other side cook for about 2 minutes, so both sides are a deep, golden brown color. As each batch is finished, place the cakes on the lined baking sheet and keep warm in the oven as you cook the rest of the cakes.

When ready to serve, spread a heaping teaspoon of the labneh mixture on each socca cake. Top with about ¼ cup cooked fennel and garnish with a few sprigs of fresh fennel fronds.

PICKLED FIG, PISTACHIO & RICOTTA CANAPÉS

MAKES ABOUT 24 MINI TARTINES

I first discovered this flavor combination on a tartine at Cyril's, the sultry, candlelit wine and cheese bar my friends Sasha and Michael opened in Portland, Oregon. I entered the restaurant sighing with happiness, leaving the gray chilling-my-bones weather at the door, and my eyes turned to saucers when I spotted these gorgeous purple, green, and white darlings on the marble bar counter. Upon first bite my mind was sent aflurry on how I might re-create, modify, and enhance this sensual little snack for my own impromptu fetes. Many a good idea has been born at the behest of a cozy space, the company of pals, and the perfect bite to eat, right?

PICKLED FIGS

12 dried Black Mission figs, sliced into thin disks

1 cup red wine vinegar

1/4 cup sugar

3 sprigs fresh thyme

CANAPÉS

1 cup whole-milk ricotta cheese

24 of your favorite crackers (I like large, circular wheat crackers)

Olive oil

Sea salt

Honey, for drizzling

1/2 cup pistachios, lightly crushed

Fresh thyme leaves, for garnish

MAKE THE PICKLED FIGS: In a small pot, combine the figs, vinegar, sugar, thyme, and 1/2 cup water and bring to a simmer over medium-low heat, about 5 minutes. Remove from the heat, cover, and let the figs steep for 2 hours or overnight in the fridge.

ASSEMBLE THE CANAPÉS: Spread about 1 heaping teaspoon of ricotta on each cracker. Gingerly place the pickled figs (about 1 or 2 per cracker) atop the ricotta, then top with olive oil, sea salt, a drizzle of honey, and a hefty sprinkle of crushed pistachios. Finish with fresh thyme leaves and serve immediately.

This combination was created as a nibble before a big family pizza night a few years ago—I had just finished a shoot for a Mexican cheese company and had pounds of different cheeses stuffed into my crisper drawer. I had gone through my initial repertoire—chilaquiles, tacos, egg scrambles, and salads—using myriad leftover cheeses when genius struck: I veered hard left and used Cotija (my favorite of the cheeses) in a completely different application, sprinkled onto lavash crackers with apricot jam and fresh rosemary from my garden. The results were positively moreish (as in gimme more!), totally addictive, and dead simple to prepare in 5 minutes. With a homemade salty margarita, these little cheesy sweet and savory snacks are heavenly. I love using ingredients from different cultures in nontraditional ways and seeing what turns up!

COTIJA, APRICOT & ROSEMARY CRISPS

SERVES 2

12 lavash crackers

2 tablespoons apricot jam

¼ cup crumbled Cotija cheese

Leaves from 1 sprig fresh rosemary, finely chopped, with 12 individual leaves reserved

Freshly cracked black pepper

Preheat the broiler. Line a baking sheet with parchment paper.

Spread the crackers on the baking sheet. Spread ½ teaspoon apricot jam evenly onto each cracker and top with 1 teaspoon Cotija cheese. Sprinkle the chopped rosemary evenly over all of the crackers, then finish each one with a rosemary leaf in the center of the cracker.

Broil the crackers for 2 minutes, or until golden brown and bubbling a bit. Garnish with a few cracks of black pepper. Serve immediately.

CHARD EMPANADAS WITH PISTACHIO CREMA

MAKES 8 TO 10 EMPANADAS

A few years ago, I was lucky enough to go on a wine trip through the vineyards of Mendoza, Argentina. Each evening, I'd whet my appetite with an empanada accompanied by a large glass of bright Torrontés wine. Some of the empanadas were fried, others baked in a wood-fired oven . . . and all were *divina*. When I got home, I went on a mad empanada bender, devising various fillings (jam and cheese, oh yes!) and riffs on dough. That's how I came upon my favorite combination, a bed of soft greens with currants bursting forth. The pistachio crema is lighter than air, a verdant ode to summer. They're Hot Pockets gone crazy, and though making them is an involved process, they're well worth the effort.

DOUGH

¾ cup all-purpose flour, plus more for rolling the dough

½ cup whole wheat flour

½ teaspoon fine sea salt

10 tablespoons unsalted butter, cut into ½-inch cubes and frozen

3 tablespoons heavy (whipping) cream

2 tablespoons ice-cold water

FILLING

2 tablespoons olive oil

1 medium red onion, diced

1 (1-pound) bunch rainbow chard, including stems, cut into ½-inch-wide ribbons/pieces

1 teaspoon grated lemon zest

1 tablespoon lemon juice

¼ cup dried currants

⅓ cup white wine

PREPARE THE DOUGH: In a food processor, pulse together the all-purpose flour, whole wheat flour, and salt. Add the butter and pulse until the butter breaks down into pea-size pieces. Pour in the cream and ice water, then pulse a few more times until you have a very sandy mixture (don't worry if it's not all sticking together). Turn the mixture out onto a smooth, dry surface and compress it into a round disk. Wrap in plastic and refrigerate for at least 30 minutes, and up to 1 week.

COOK THE FILLING: In a large skillet, heat the olive oil over medium heat. Add the red onion and sauté until the onion becomes soft and slightly translucent, about 5 minutes. Add the chard, lemon zest, lemon juice, currants, and wine and cook until the leaves have wilted and the liquids have reduced, 5 to 6 minutes. Stir in the nutmeg, garlic, and salt and pepper to taste. Pour the greens into a medium bowl until ready for filling.

MAKE THE PISTACHIO CREMA: In a blender, combine the parsley, mint, salt, pistachios, lemon juice, and water and blend on high speed until smooth. (If the crema is too thick, add an additional ¼ cup water and blend.) Transfer to a medium bowl. Cover and refrigerate until ready to serve.

(continued)

note Place formed, unbaked empanadas on a baking sheet and freeze for about 4 hours, then transfer them to a plastic bag and keep them in the freezer for an impromptu tapas-themed evening. Just add a couple of minutes to the baking time.

⅛ teaspoon freshly grated
nutmeg

1 large garlic clove, minced

Fine sea salt and freshly ground
black pepper

PISTACHIO CREMA

½ bunch flat-leaf parsley, leaves
roughly chopped

1 bunch fresh mint

Pinch of sea salt

1 cup salted roasted pistachios
(you can toast and salt yourself
or use store-bought)

2 tablespoons lemon juice

¼ cup water

1 large egg

1 tablespoon heavy (whipping)
cream

Lemon wedges, for squeezing

10 fresh mint leaves, for garnish

10 flat-leaf parsley leaves, for
garnish

MAKE THE EMPANADAS: Preheat the oven to 375°F.
Line 2 baking sheets with parchment paper.

On a heavily floured surface, roll out the dough to about a
¼-inch thickness, flipping the dough and reflouring the surface
and rolling pin after each couple of passes. Use a drinking glass
or a cookie cutter to cut out 4-inch rounds of dough. (Gather
the scraps and place in the fridge while you stuff the rounds that
have been cut out. Then reroll and cut out more rounds—you
should end up with about 10 rounds of dough.)

Place about 2 heaping tablespoons of filling on one half of a
dough round, then fold the dough in half, pressing lightly with
your fingers and then using the tines of a fork to really seal the
edges and create a cute design. (Be careful not to overstuff or
else the pastry will fall apart—if there is leftover filling, enjoy it
with a fried egg or stirred into couscous or rice.) Transfer the
finished empanadas to the lined pans and poke each empanada
with a fork 2 to 3 times to allow steam to escape when baking.

In a small bowl, beat the egg with the cream. Brush the mixture
generously over each empanada. Bake the empanadas, rotating
the pans front to back midway through for even browning, for 20
to 25 minutes, until very golden brown. Let cool on the pan for 5
minutes, or up to 1 hour.

Serve with a dollop of pistachio crema and lemon wedges.
Garnish with a few mint and parsley leaves.

TOASTED NUTS WITH LEMON, THYME & CHILI

SERVES 4 TO 6

Having a few deliciously fragrant mixed nuts with a cup of tea (or whiskey!) just hits the spot sometimes. These nuts come together quickly on the stove top and make an excellent nibble on their own or as part of a cheese plate. I incorporated a favorite flavor combination of lemon and thyme and added zing with a smidge of chili powder and brown sugar—the resulting sweet, savory, salty, and spicy mixed nuts are divinely addictive.

2½ cups mixed raw nuts

2 tablespoons unsalted butter

2 tablespoons light brown sugar

1 teaspoon fresh thyme leaves

1 teaspoon grated lemon zest

½ teaspoon chili powder

½ teaspoon fine sea salt

Line a baking sheet with parchment.

In a large skillet, heat the nuts over medium-low heat, stirring occasionally, until aromatic and slightly toasted, about 20 minutes (low heat is key to a nice even toasting). When the nuts are toasted, add the butter, brown sugar, thyme, lemon zest, chili powder, and salt and toss to coat the nuts lightly with the spice mixture. Cook, stirring constantly, until the nuts are completely candied, 2 to 3 minutes longer. Pour onto the lined baking sheet to cool for at least 5 minutes. These can be kept in a sealed container at room temperature for up to 5 days.

POTLUCKS & PICNICS

let's eat!

What can I bring? Are there any sweeter words to hear when organizing a little get-together? The beauty of communal eating events is how easy they are to pull together: Friends and family are invited to collaborate over delicious food to contribute so that everyone—even the host—can bask in one another's company. Throwing a potluck or picnic is a host's best secret. Don't do it all yourself; ask friends to bring their favorite dish and fill in the menu with a few of your top choices. I never mind a little overlap in foods; it's more about the merriment of coming together and whiling away a few hours. And for those friends who don't cook, allow them to pick up a dish from their favorite neighborhood restaurant.

When it comes to picnicking, you really only need a blanket, a patch of sand or grass, bubbly water, and a good salad (may I recommend Kale Slaw with Breadcrumbs, Lemon & Ricotta Salata on page 127). Anything else is gravy. It's the most basic of all eating joys and can offer a natural respite from an ordinary workday or be the highlight of a weekend gathering.

And potlucks can be the most casual affair of all—with friends hanging out on lawns and hammocks, drinking coffee and mimosas in the sunshine, until dishes like Blooming Flower Salads (page 124) and Butterscotch Pots de Crème (page 140) are all gone, the day has faded away completely, and you're suddenly inside cuddled up in blankets watching a movie and making Turkish Red Lentil Soup (page 135). Let's all feast; I'm pretty sure these are the salad days.

Warmed Olives,
page 114

Smoky Delicata Squash
with Pecorino, *page 115*

It's beguiling how so few ingredients, when met with a touch of heat and a pretty plate, can become an elevated snack fit for a queen. A savory bite that always hits the spot, these olives are the ideal excuse to while away an afternoon with a dear friend, sharing secrets, laughter, and a bottle of red. I keep most of these ingredients in my fridge and pantry at all times, proving it never hurts to have a quick appetizer on hand for impromptu fun or while you're finishing dinner for guests.

WARMED OLIVES

MAKES ABOUT 1¼ CUPS

1 cup Castelvetrano olives

¼ cup Marcona almonds

2 garlic cloves, smashed with the side of a knife

1 wide strip of lemon zest

2 tablespoons olive oil

¼ teaspoon dried oregano

¼ teaspoon red pepper flakes

Fine sea salt and freshly ground black pepper

In a small saucepan, combine the ingredients and cook over medium heat for about 5 minutes to heat through. Toss the mixture a few times and serve immediately in a shallow bowl.

SMOKY DELICATA SQUASH WITH PECORINO

SERVES 2

My love for delicata squash blossomed during the autumns we spent living in Portland, Oregon. It's a vegetable I had never had growing up in Southern California, but David, my husband, is a squash addict. Every Saturday morning at the farmers' market, he'd make a beeline for the prettiest delicatas, and, inevitably, we'd be having a squash fest hours later for lunch. So easy and quick to cook, and so reliably tasty, it makes a hearty snack and continues to be the basis of many meals for us.

---

2 tablespoons olive oil

1 large delicata squash, skin on, seeded and cut into ¼-inch slices (about 3 cups)

Fine sea salt and freshly ground black pepper

¼ teaspoon smoked paprika

¼ cup finely shredded pecorino cheese

1 teaspoon fresh oregano leaves

In a large skillet, heat the olive oil over medium-high heat until it shimmers. Add the delicata squash and a pinch each of salt and pepper. Cook, stirring often, for 8 to 10 minutes, until the squash is slightly tender when pierced with a fork. Add the paprika and 2 tablespoons water. Cover the pan and cook for 2 minutes longer to let the squash steam. Uncover and shake the pan for 30 seconds more to coat everything evenly.

Transfer the steamed squash to a serving dish and top with the pecorino and fresh oregano leaves.

SWEET POTATO TORTILLA ESPAÑOLA

SERVES 8

¼ cup olive oil

2 to 3 medium sweet potatoes, peeled and cut into ½-inch cubes (about 4 cups)

½ medium white onion, thinly sliced (½ cup)

5 large eggs

½ teaspoon fine sea salt, plus more for garnish

Freshly ground black pepper, for garnish

Fresh thyme sprigs, for garnish

note This iteration is made with sweet potatoes, a veer away from the white potatoes used in Spain. I love the delicate flavor and bright orange of sweet potatoes, and I often make this dish when I need a nourishing meal but the fridge is mostly empty.

When my Spanish host mother first met sixteen-year-old me, I had just breezed into her small, walk-up apartment in Seville with plastic platform flip-flops, a hot pink tube top, pierced tongue, and an adamant vegetarianism attitude (it was the '90s!). "*No jamón?*" she inquired with utter shock, discontent, disdain, and sadness in her eyes. Indeed no jamón, oxtail stew, or tuna fish pie—that was my response each time she served something from the omnipresent meat-driven meals. But we tolerated each other, the summer rolled on, and soon we found common ground with the tortilla—a wonderfully simple vegetarian creation and favorite anytime snack or light meal.

A tortilla is traditionally a large potato cake, flavored with a little egg, salt, pepper, and onion. It's the perfect dish for tapas: It can be cut into small wedges or little squares, goes nicely with beer or wine, and is good at room temperature, though best hot off the skillet. As I discovered that summer, a slice of tortilla even travels well if tucked into a napkin for later enjoyment.

In a 10-inch nonstick or cast-iron skillet, heat the olive oil over medium heat. Add the sweet potatoes and onion and cook until tender, about 10 minutes, stirring every minute or so to prevent sticking. Pour the sweet potatoes and onion into a sieve set over a large bowl. Measure out 1 tablespoon of the oil and return to the skillet (reserve the remaining drained oil for another use; it's delicious brushed onto morning toast or bagels). Return the sweet potatoes and onion to the skillet.

In a medium bowl, whisk together the eggs and the ½ teaspoon salt until combined.

Spread the sweet potatoes and onion into an even layer. Pour the eggs on top of the potatoes. Use a spatula to push the eggs through any cracks in the vegetables, but do not stir—or else you will not form one uniform mound. Cook over medium-low heat for 5 minutes, then cover the pan and cook until the eggs are mostly set, 5 to 7 minutes longer. Remove from the heat and allow the tortilla to rest, with the cover on, for another 5 minutes, to help the center set (this way there's no flipping required).

Run a spatula around the edges of the tortilla in the pan. Place a platter or a cutting board on top of the pan, then invert the pan to release the tortilla, golden-side up, onto the platter. Flip it again to show the sweet potato side facing up. Garnish with a little extra salt, plenty of black pepper, and a smattering of thyme leaves and sprigs.

SPRING GREEN COUSCOUS CUPS

SERVES 6

I have an unabashed love of a good pasta or grain salad dressed in saucy vinaigrette. I eat some variation on this theme almost every day. These couscous cups are my favorite manifestation of this simple, nourishing idea—they are a celebration of all things emerald, from the bursting peas to the verdant kale pesto to the pistachios and scallions dancing across the tops. It's a parade of texture, health, and goodness, a party fit for springtime.

Fine sea salt

2 cups Israeli couscous

1 cup frozen or shelled fresh green peas

¾ cup roughly chopped raw pistachios

3 scallions, chopped

1 cup Kale Pesto (page 201)

2 cups chopped butter lettuce

6 teaspoons lemon juice

1 tablespoon olive oil

Freshly ground black pepper

Lemon wedges, for squeezing

Shaved Parmesan, for garnish

Fill a medium pot with water and bring to a boil. Add salt until it tastes briny like the ocean. When the water returns to a rolling boil, add the couscous and boil until al dente, about 7 minutes. Add the peas and cook for 1 minute longer. Drain the couscous and peas in a colander and run under a stream of cold water to stop the cooking process.

Transfer the couscous and peas to a medium bowl. Add the pistachios, scallions, and ½ cup of the pesto and toss until the couscous is well coated.

In a small bowl, toss together the lettuce, 2 teaspoons of the lemon juice, and the olive oil.

Add the remaining 4 teaspoons lemon juice to the couscous mixture and taste to adjust for seasoning, adding more salt and pepper.

To assemble, arrange a small handful of butter lettuce in each serving bowl. Place ½ cup of the couscous mixture in each bowl atop the lettuce. Finish with a tablespoon of pesto in each, and serve with lemon wedges and a few shavings of Parmesan.

BEETS IN COCONUT WITH CURRY LEAVES

SERVES 4

Here's a dish as beautiful to behold as it is delicious to eat. Subtly exotic with the addition of fresh, aromatic curry leaves and velvety sweet coconut milk, these beets look like sparkling gemstones floating atop a tinted pool of bright color and flavor. Even if you don't think you have an artistic bone in your body, this stunning snack will make you look like a master painter, with the most vivid of palettes displayed on the plate. This warm, soupy salad can be transformed into a full-on meal when paired with some fresh Peshwari naan or poured over a bowl of basmati rice.

2 bunches beets (about 10), trimmed of their leaves

2 tablespoons coconut oil

1 teaspoon mustard seeds

1 teaspoon ground cumin

2 shallots, sliced

12 fresh curry leaves (see Note)

1 cup coconut milk

Juice of 2 limes

Fine sea salt and freshly ground black pepper

Lime wedges, for serving

Preheat the oven to 400°F.

Wrap the beets loosely in foil, crimping the edges so the beets are sealed shut. Bake for 40 minutes, or until tender when pierced with a fork. Remove them from the foil packets and place in a medium bowl to cool. When cool enough to handle, rub the skins loose and discard, then cut the beets into slim wedges. Arrange the beet wedges on a plate.

In a medium saucepan, heat the coconut oil over medium-high heat until it shimmers. Add the mustard seeds, cumin, shallots, and curry leaves and stir until fragrant, 4 to 5 minutes. Add the coconut milk and cook until warmed through, about 2 minutes. Pour over the arranged beets.

Add the lime juice and a sprinkling of salt and pepper. Garnish with a few extra lime wedges and serve immediately.

note Curry leaves are available at most Indian and Asian groceries.

TUNISIAN EGG PITA WITH HARISSA, DILL & CUMIN CARROTS

SERVES 4

I locked eyes with a version of this sandwich in the cart of a bustling market in Tunis, the capital city of Tunisia. After a day of helping schlep camera equipment, take notes, and unveil Polaroids for my father as he documented the architectural ruins just outside the city center, I was getting "hangry" and approaching madness. This street food sandwich was my oasis: A pillowy pita was punctuated by a familiar hard-boiled egg, cumin-scented carrots, bright dill, and pickled shallots, all bathed in harissa, the spicy signature condiment of the country. After a little experimenting, I present my own take on this satisfying, electric little snack, good for a picnic or beach trip with friends, or solo at the kitchen counter, daydreaming about another exotic locale.

4 medium carrots, quartered

1 tablespoon olive oil, plus more for drizzling

½ teaspoon ground cumin

Fine sea salt

Harissa

⅓ cup whole-milk Greek yogurt

2 pita breads, halved

4 large hard-boiled eggs, roughly chopped

Fresh dill sprigs

Quick Pickled Shallots (recipe follows)

Freshly ground black pepper

Preheat the oven to 425°F. Line a baking sheet with parchment paper.

In a bowl, toss the carrots with the 1 tablespoon olive oil, the cumin, and a pinch of salt. Spread the carrots evenly on the baking sheet and roast for 15 minutes, or until slightly soft and browned on the edges.

Mix a few small dots of harissa into the yogurt, then taste and adjust the harissa amount. When spiced to your preference, smear a tablespoon on each side of the pita halves. Divide the chopped eggs evenly among the pitas. Tuck 4 pieces of carrot into each pita. Top with 3 or 4 dill sprigs and a small handful of pickled shallots. Drizzle the sandwich fillings with a generous amount of olive oil. Finish with a few more shallots, and season with salt and pepper to taste. Serve immediately.

QUICK PICKLED SHALLOTS

MAKES ½ CUP

¼ cup white wine vinegar

2 tablespoons sugar

Fine sea salt

2 shallots, sliced as thinly as possible

MAKE THE PICKLED SHALLOTS: In a small bowl, whisk together the vinegar, sugar, and a pinch of salt. Stir the shallots into the vinegar mixture. Pour the shallots and liquid into a small jar, then cover and let sit for at least 30 minutes, or up to 1 week in the fridge.

BLOOMING FLOWER SALADS

SERVES 2

Did you know there's a plethora of flowers you can eat, as well as enjoy in a bouquet? Once you know which are edible, you can easily add them to your culinary repertoire, seeking them out at farmers' markets or growing a few yourself to toss into salads or scatter on top of a cake. The flowers called for in this fairy-tale salad are largely available at most farmers' markets, nurseries, or occasionally at fancy grocery stores sold in containers labeled "edible flowers." But if you're buying outside of your supermarket, make sure you ask an informed attendant about how the flowers are grown and treated. Try to eat these salads without smiling ear to ear—it's an impossible feat!

2 tablespoons olive oil

2 tablespoons white wine vinegar

1 teaspoon honey

1 garlic clove, minced

Sea salt and freshly ground black pepper

3 cups arugula, stems trimmed

3 medium radishes, thinly sliced

1 medium carrot, peeled into ribbons

1 cup organic, untreated petals from the following flowers, in an assortment of colors: 1 rose, 3 chrysanthemums, 3 calendula flowers, 3 cosmos flowers, 6 nasturtium flowers

In a large wooden bowl, whisk together the olive oil, vinegar, honey, garlic, and salt and pepper to taste until well combined. Toss the arugula, radishes, and carrot ribbons with the dressing in the bowl.

Divide the salads between 2 plates. Scatter all the flower petals on top of the vegetable mixture and serve immediately.

KALE SLAW WITH BREADCRUMBS, LEMON & RICOTTA SALATA

SERVES 4 TO 6

¼ cup olive oil

½ cup lemon juice

1 tablespoon white wine vinegar

Fine sea salt and freshly ground black pepper

1 bunch Lacinato kale, stems removed and leaves cut into thin ribbons

10 medium radishes, thinly sliced

1 cup croutons

5 ounces ricotta salata, shaved with a vegetable peeler

This is one of my favorite salads—I could eat the whole bowl for lunch. It's great as is, or as a bed for avocado slices or grilled tofu. It travels well, too, as the flavors really meld when left at room temperature for a couple of hours before eating. I'm amazed at how the sharp tastes of radishes and salty ricotta salata totally mellow with the dressing and complement the kale.

In a large wooden bowl, whisk together the olive oil, lemon juice, vinegar, and a pinch each of salt and pepper. Add the kale and radishes and toss with the dressing. Massage with the dressing for about 1 minute, squeezing between your fingers to help mellow the sharpness of the radishes and the bite of the kale.

In a mortar, crush the croutons with a pestle until they are the size of large breadcrumbs. Toss the ricotta salata and breadcrumbs into the salad to finish.

note Once you get the basic formula down for a tangy dressing with the kale sliced thin, you can endlessly riff on toppings according to your preference and what you have on hand—toasted nuts, dried fruits, fresh fruits, grains, and other cheeses are all wonderful crowd-pleasers should you care to deviate from the original recipe here.

CHOPPED RADICCHIO SALAD

SERVES 4

This salad has been a staple for me since I tasted a version of it at Portland's most popular restaurant, Toro Bravo. I've sassed up my version with even more little morsels—from green olives to white beans, bits of parsley and candied walnuts—so eating becomes a veritable treasure hunt amid the bitter purple leaves. This vegetarian mélange is a sustaining yet light picnic lunch.

3 tablespoons olive oil

3 tablespoons white wine vinegar

1 tablespoon mayonnaise

1 garlic clove, finely minced

Fine sea salt and freshly ground black pepper

1 head radicchio (about ¾ pound), trimmed and roughly chopped

½ cup green olives, pitted and roughly chopped

1 heaping cup cooked white beans (such as navy or cannellini)

½ cup halved, thinly sliced red onion

½ cup thinly sliced pecorino cheese, plus more for serving

1 cup chopped fresh flat-leaf parsley

1 small green apple, julienned

1 teaspoon unsalted butter

½ cup walnuts, roughly chopped

1 tablespoon light brown sugar

In the bottom of a large salad bowl, whisk together the olive oil, vinegar, mayonnaise, garlic, and salt and pepper to taste until the dressing is emulsified. Add the radicchio, olives, beans, onion, pecorino, parsley, and apple to the salad bowl and toss with the dressing.

In a medium skillet, melt the butter over medium heat. Add the walnuts, brown sugar, and a pinch of salt and stir until the nuts are evenly coated and the brown sugar has mostly melted onto the walnuts, about 4 minutes.

Add the candied nuts to the salad and toss thoroughly. Serve with extra pecorino on the side.

note This salad is even better after a few hours in the fridge, so you can put it together and then get ready before meeting friends at the park.

BUBBLING SAVORY OATS WITH BROCCOLI & COTSWOLD CHEESE

SERVES 6

1 cup oat groats

3 cups vegetable broth

3 cups roughly chopped broccoli florets and stalks

2 tablespoons olive oil

1 tablespoon unsalted butter

1 leek, white part only, roughly chopped

1 garlic clove, minced

¼ cup white wine

⅓ cup heavy (whipping) cream

½ cup roughly chopped fresh chives

½ teaspoon grated lemon zest

Pinch of fine sea salt

1½ cups shredded Cotswold cheese

Freshly ground black pepper

Oat groats are the nutty and nubby star of these little pots. I love them because they have all the flavor of oatmeal, but retain a bouncy texture and individual, oblong shape. When folded into a hearty mixture of leeks, classic British cheese, and roasted broccoli, they become the vehicle for all the other tasty add-ins. When the sun starts setting earlier come fall and winter, I reach for this cheesy little pot of goodness. You can assemble these personal-size casseroles ahead of time and bake them at a friend's house for a cozy contribution to a potluck.

In a medium pot, combine the oat groats and vegetable broth and bring to a boil. Reduce the heat to a simmer and cook for 50 minutes until the groats are tender, stirring occasionally.

Meanwhile, preheat the oven to 400°F. Line a baking sheet with parchment.

Toss the broccoli in the olive oil directly on the parchment-lined pan. Roast the broccoli for about 15 minutes, or until just tender and crispy on the edges. Set aside. Leave the oven on.

In a medium saucepan, melt the butter over medium heat. Add the leek and garlic and cook until the leek softens, 4 to 5 minutes. Add the wine, cream, ¼ cup of the chives, the lemon zest, and salt and cook for 1 minute.

Drain the cooked oat groats and place in a large bowl. Mix in the broccoli and the leek mixture, and stir in 1 cup of the Cotswold cheese. Divide the mixture among six 5-ounce ramekins, topping each with a sprinkle of the remaining ½ cup cheese. Place the ramekins on a baking sheet and bake for about 5 minutes. Turn on the broiler and broil for 2 minutes to finish and to get the cheese really bubbling.

To serve, top each ramekin with a sprinkle of the remaining ¼ cup of chives and the freshly ground pepper.

POLENTA WITH BLISTERED TOMATOES, WALNUTS & THYME

SERVES 4

There's a special subtle power to polenta. It's made from such a humble ingredient, cornmeal, yet after a little boiling and delicate stirring, it transforms into something silky, rib-sticking, and utterly satisfying. I don't know a problem a warm bowl of this golden sunshine can't cure: It's the perfect base to whatever exciting ingredients you throw at it. In the evenings, try it beneath a chunky stew or braised winter greens; in the mornings, below a fried egg or chopped nuts and herbs. For a low-key gathering, I especially love it against the burst of sweetness from cherry tomatoes, the earthy tones of toasted walnuts, and a dollop of tangy yogurt.

2 cups cherry tomatoes

1 tablespoon plus 1 teaspoon olive oil, plus more for drizzling

Fine sea salt and freshly ground black pepper

4 sprigs fresh thyme

½ cup walnuts, roughly chopped

1 cup polenta or yellow cornmeal

Pinch of nutmeg

½ cup finely shredded Parmesan cheese, plus more for garnish

1 tablespoon unsalted butter

¼ cup plain whole-milk yogurt

Preheat the oven to 400°F. Line a baking sheet with parchment paper.

In a small bowl, toss together the cherry tomatoes, 1 tablespoon of the olive oil, and salt and pepper to taste. Spread the tomatoes on the baking sheet in an even layer, add 3 sprigs of the thyme, and bake for 20 minutes, or until the tomatoes are blistered and soft. Set aside.

In a medium nonstick skillet, heat the remaining 1 teaspoon olive oil over medium-low heat. Add the walnuts and a pinch of salt and cook, stirring constantly, until the walnuts are toasty in color and aromatic, 3 or 4 minutes. Transfer the walnuts to a plate to cool.

In a medium pot, bring 3 cups water to a boil. Add the polenta and pinch of nutmeg, reduce the heat to medium-low, and cook, whisking the entire time, until the water is absorbed and the polenta is cooked through, about 6 minutes. Remove from the heat and stir in the Parmesan and butter. Season with salt and pepper to taste.

Scoop ½-cup portions of polenta into 4 bowls. Dress each bowl with 1 tablespoon yogurt, 2 tablespoons walnuts, ½ cup of the tomatoes, and the thyme leaves from the remaining sprig. Garnish each bowl with extra Parmesan and a drizzle of olive oil. Serve warm.

note To make this ahead for a group hangout, you can spread the polenta onto a parchment-lined and greased baking sheet, let cool for 20 minutes, and top with all the toppings scattered messily about. Remove from the pan and cut into bite-size squares.

note I top this soup with sumac, a lemony tasting spice made of ground berries found in North Africa and all over the Middle East. You can find it at specialty spice shops and Middle Eastern groceries.

TURKISH RED LENTIL SOUP

SERVES 4 TO 6

We spent a winter in Istanbul a few years back, and nothing could have prepared me for the sheer glory and audacity of this city. The spices, architecture, pastries, and bustle were enchanting beyond compare. After all that daily exploration, we often sought comfort at our neighborhood kebab shop in a bowl of red lentil soup. When you're very far away from all that is familiar, there's something deeply satisfying about ordering a bowl of nourishing soup, and this dish needed no adornment other than an extra squeeze of lemon and a basket of baguette slices to do the job of sopping up.

Soups are especially communal, being cooked throughout the world in big aluminum pots, simmering all day with hardly a stir. Best of all, it's a no-muss food—in Istanbul we ordered what all the commuters seemed to be getting, as they know what's delicious (and fast!). My take here is pretty dead-on from that first taste in Istanbul. It's earthy and bright, energizing but soothing—much like the city that inspired it—and a study in opposites in its high flavor contrast.

2 tablespoons olive oil

½ medium onion, diced

1 medium carrot, diced

4 garlic cloves, minced

1 teaspoon smoked paprika

1 heaping tablespoon dried mint

¼ teaspoon cayenne pepper

Fine sea salt and freshly ground black pepper

1 cup red lentils

5 cups vegetable stock

2 tablespoons tomato paste

Juice of 1 lemon

Sumac, for garnish (see Note, page 134)

Lemon wedges, for serving

In a large pot, heat the oil over medium heat. Add the onion, carrot, garlic, paprika, mint, cayenne, and salt and black pepper to taste. Cook until the carrots and onion soften, about 4 minutes. Stir in the lentils, stock, and tomato paste and bring to a boil. Reduce to a simmer and cook until the lentils are tender, about 20 minutes. Remove from the heat.

Stir the lemon juice into the soup. Puree the soup with an immersion blender right in the pot (or in batches in a stand blender) until mostly smooth with a few remaining chunks. (Take care to avoid splashes of hot soup.)

Ladle the soup into bowls. Garnish each with salt and black pepper and a sprinkling of sumac. Serve with lemon wedges.

GREEN PEA & SPINACH SOUP WITH CHIVES, YOGURT & NIGELLA

SERVES 4 TO 6

1 tablespoon olive oil, plus more for drizzling

1 medium onion, roughly chopped

1 garlic clove, minced

6 cups frozen peas

4 cups fresh spinach

1½ cups coconut milk

4 cups vegetable broth

2 teaspoons fine sea salt

Juice of 1 lemon

Whole-milk yogurt, for garnish

Chopped fresh chives, for garnish

Nigella seeds, for garnish (see Note)

There's something about blended soups that makes me feel so polished, refined, and ladylike—they feel very pure, simple, and French. In this version of pea soup, gone is the stodgy, mealy canned version, and in its place a light, balanced, and graceful expression of fresh spring flavors. This soup is not cooked for long and is very fast to prepare, perfect for a last-minute get-together. It uses easy freezer and pantry staples (peas and coconut milk) and finishes with a pretty garnish of chives and nigella seeds. A different herb, such as basil or parsley, chopped walnuts, or even a scattering of feta or goat cheese would be superb here as well.

In a heavy-bottomed soup pot, heat the 1 tablespoon olive oil over medium heat. Add the onion and garlic and cook until softened, about 5 minutes. Add the peas, spinach, coconut milk, vegetable broth, salt, and lemon juice and let the mixture come to a light boil.

Immediately remove the pot from the heat. Puree the soup with an immersion blender right in the pot (or in batches in a stand blender) until mostly smooth. (Take care to avoid splashes of hot soup.)

Ladle into bowls and garnish each with a swirl of yogurt, a sprinkling of chives, a drizzle of olive oil, and a sprinkling of nigella seeds.

note Nigella seeds are commonly found in Middle Eastern groceries or specialty spice stores. They have a very distinctive savory flavor and add a lot of punch to breads, legumes, and salads.

HAZELNUT TEA CAKE WITH PLUMS

MAKES ONE 9-INCH CAKE

Who doesn't love a great tea cake? This simple but splendid little quick bread is commonly served at home in France and England. It's mellow and satisfying in a way that fancy tiers of cake covered with icing and ganache, with all their bells and whistles, are not. This recipe is also great with almond or cashew meal, but I find that ground hazelnut has a richness and an earthy character. Serve this cake with whatever fruit is peaking with sweetness: I love juicy plums for summer and early fall.

CAKE

⅓ cup olive oil, plus more for greasing the pan

1 cup plus 2 tablespoons ground hazelnuts

½ cup whole-milk ricotta cheese

4 ounces cream cheese, at room temperature

¾ cup granulated sugar

2 large eggs

1 teaspoon vanilla extract

1 tablespoon Drambuie (Cointreau or your favorite citrus liqueur would also work)

⅔ cup all-purpose flour

1½ teaspoons baking powder

½ teaspoon baking soda

½ teaspoon fine sea salt

PLUM TOPPING

1 tablespoon unsalted butter

4 medium plums, cut into ¼-inch wedges

2 tablespoons light brown sugar

Pinch of fine sea salt

2 tablespoons ground hazelnuts

Edible nasturtium flowers, for garnish (optional)

MAKE THE CAKE: Preheat the oven to 375°F. Grease a 9-inch cake pan with enough oil to evenly coat the pan's interior. Dust the sides with 2 tablespoons of the ground hazelnuts.

In the bowl of an electric stand mixer fitted with the whisk attachment, beat together the ricotta, cream cheese, granulated sugar, and the ⅓ cup olive oil until light and fluffy. Add the eggs, vanilla, and Drambuie and mix until evenly incorporated.

In a medium bowl, whisk together the remaining 1 cup ground hazelnuts, the flour, baking powder, baking soda, and salt. Add the hazelnut mixture to the ricotta mixture, mixing until just combined. Pour the batter into the cake pan and bake for 35 to 40 minutes, until golden brown and a toothpick inserted in the center of the cake comes out clean. Remove the cake from the pan and let cool on a wire rack.

PREPARE THE TOPPING: When ready to serve, plate the cake on a pretty platter or cake stand. In a medium saucepan, heat the butter over medium-high heat. Add the plums, brown sugar, and salt. Cook until the plums are soft but not mushy, about 5 minutes.

Pour the warm plum mixture on top of the cake. Sprinkle the ground hazelnuts on top of the plums. If desired, scatter a few nasturtium flowers on top. Cut into wedges and serve immediately. Store any leftover cake and plums covered in the fridge for 2 to 3 days.

BUTTERSCOTCH POTS DE CRÈME WITH TOASTED CORNBREAD CROUTONS

SERVES 6

The French *pot de crème* is a traditional custard hardly in need of an introduction, but I've given it a bit of an American upgrade by adding salt and dark brown sugar, and topping the whole thing with cubes of cornbread toasted in browned butter. These decadent treats travel well and can be made ahead of time. The combination of butter, cream, and egg yolks shouts a message of pure indulgence loud and clear. So listen up: When all you want is that sweet and salty combination, this dessert totally delivers.

TOPPING

2 teaspoons coconut oil

2 teaspoons unsalted butter

1½ cups cornbread cubes (1-inch), with any crumbs

1 teaspoon dark brown sugar

¼ teaspoon fine sea salt

POTS DE CRÈME

1½ cups heavy (whipping) cream

½ cup packed dark brown sugar

¼ teaspoon fine sea salt

1 vanilla bean, halved lengthwise

4 large egg yolks

½ teaspoon vanilla extract

Powdered sugar, for garnish

MAKE THE TOPPING: In a large skillet, melt the coconut oil and butter over medium heat. Add the cornbread cubes, brown sugar, and salt and cook, stirring occasionally, until the cornbread takes on a toasty smell and a golden brown color, 5 to 7 minutes. (It's fine if the croutons become crumbly during the cooking process!) Pour the browned cornbread onto a plate lined with paper towels and set aside.

PREPARE THE POTS DE CRÈME: Preheat the oven to 325°F. In a saucepan, combine the cream, 6 tablespoons of the brown sugar, and salt. Scrape in the vanilla seeds and add the vanilla pod. Bring to a simmer. Remove from the heat, cover, and let steep for 15 minutes. Remove the vanilla pod and discard. Set the vanilla cream aside.

In a medium glass or metal bowl, whisk the egg yolks and vanilla extract until combined. Set aside.

In a heavy-bottomed saucepan, combine 6 tablespoons water and the remaining 2 tablespoons brown sugar over medium-high heat. Swirl the pan to dissolve the sugar, but do not stir with a spoon or whisk, or the mixture may crystallize. Let the sugar cook for 5 minutes, until the liquid bubbles away, leaving a pure caramel behind, then remove the pot from the heat and whisk in the vanilla cream. Add about ¼ cup of the hot mixture to the beaten yolks, whisking vigorously. Add the remainder of the hot cream mixture to the yolks and whisk to combine.

Pour the custard mixture through a fine-mesh sieve into six 4-ounce jars or ramekins, filling each about three-fourths full. Place the jars in a 9 x 13-inch baking pan and fill with warm water three-fourths of the way to the top.

Bake the custards for 35 to 40 minutes, until they are set but still a little wobbly in the center. Remove the custards from the water bath and let cool to warm or room temperature.

To serve, top each custard with 2 heaping tablespoons of cornbread croutons and a dusting of powdered sugar.

CASHEW CRÈME WITH SEASONAL FRUITS & CACAO NIBS

SERVES 6 TO 8

Cashew crème is an enchanting substance—it's velvety and rich with a subtle elegance most desserts could only dream of. It's an easy treat to assemble at a friend's home or outside for a welcome sweet addition to a picnic. When I first made it a few years ago, my friends and I gobbled up an entire plate of it, dunking the ripest figs from a neighborhood tree into the crème in order to mop up every morsel. It was so revelatory that now this recipe is my secret weapon to satisfy all eaters—gluten-free, vegan, raw, nondairy, you name it, this dessert can make anybody happy.

2 cups raw cashews

2 dates, pitted and roughly chopped

2 tablespoons coconut oil

1 teaspoon vanilla extract

½ teaspoon fine sea salt

3 cups sliced seasonal fruit

¼ cup cacao nibs, finely chopped, for garnish

Place the cashews in a medium bowl and cover with water. Let soak overnight, then drain well.

In a high-speed blender or food processor, combine the soaked cashews, dates, coconut oil, vanilla, salt, and 1 cup water and puree until smooth.

Pour the cashew crème onto a platter and top with the seasonal fruit. Sprinkle the cacao nibs all over. Serve immediately.

note Strawberries, stone fruits, figs, and pears are great for topping the crème. And cacao nibs set off any sweet fruit with their slight bitterness and satisfying crunch.

DESSERTS

let them eat cake!

Go ahead and take up a lot of space. Be the star of the party, bring out something ridiculous, and watch the jaws drop. There is a time and place for extraordinary desserts, and I find myself tackling my most ambitious recipes on weekends when I have more time to prepare something special. My morning might start with a trip to the farmers' market to procure the juiciest fruit and then to the grocery for any other necessary items. I go hog-wild from there. If there is no fete planned by friends, I make a little party of my own design to celebrate my creation. I promise, they come in droves. It's a rather selfish act, as I love to spend the day spinning sugar into something pretty, culminating in a delicious sweetness, but I won't tell the guests if you don't.

Because the weekdays can feel so rushed, it's nice to use the weekends to revel a bit more in the act of creating—to decompress and meditate on the past week and what's to come. Nothing clears my head or solves conundrums like getting my hands in a mess of sugar, flour, chocolate, and fruit. It's the cheapest form of therapy and the results are glorious. These longer projects are not intimidating, however: The Unicones (page 171), for example, are nothing more than a happy conglomeration of store-bought sprinkles, some good ice cream cones, and a melted chocolate bar. The Blueberry Galette with Mascarpone & Oat Crust (page 159) is a cinch due to its free-form nature (no expertise or precision required for rolling out the dough). And there are a few more-lengthy endeavors to look forward to, such as the Lemon-Strawberry Tart (page 150) and the Chocolate Sandwiches with Caramel & Peanut Butter (page 148). Let's tidy up the kitchen in anticipation, put the hair into a bun, throw on our slippers, roll up our bathrobe sleeves, and get to it, shall we?

Chocolate Sandwiches with Caramel & Peanut Butter, *page 148*

As a kid, I often dreamed of opening up my lunch box to find Fruit-by-the-Foot, Gushers, or Shark Bites (any jacked-up sugary gummy would do); processed cheese and crackers hermetically sealed in excessive amounts of plastic; an ice-cold chocolate milk; and a long-winded note written by my mom about how great I was. But the reality of my lunch was a paper bag containing a natural peanut butter sandwich on whole wheat bread, with a thin layer of low-sugar jam, and a mealy apple. I had nothing to trade, dead broke in the kid economy of lunch bartering.

All this to say, these chocolate sandwiches are the stuff I would've fallen off my bench for if they'd appeared during my grade-school years. You know something cool, though? Being an adult may come with its challenges, but when you pack your lunch, you can finally make yourself chocolate sandwiches, with the centers loaded with peanut butter frosting and gobs of salty caramel if that's what you want. You can eat them with your friends, your parents, your children—they make everyone feel six years old all over again. Suddenly you're the cool kid with the crazy lunch item.

CHOCOLATE SANDWICHES WITH CARAMEL & PEANUT BUTTER

MAKES 6 SANDWICHES

CAKE

3 sticks (12 ounces) unsalted butter, plus more for greasing the pan

1 1/2 cups unsweetened cocoa powder, plus more for dusting the pan

3 cups brewed coffee

1 cup packed light brown sugar

1 cup granulated sugar

4 cups all-purpose flour

3 teaspoons baking soda

1 1/2 teaspoons fine sea salt

6 large eggs

2 teaspoons vanilla extract

PREPARE THE CAKE: Preheat the oven to 350°F. Butter a 9 x 13-inch baking pan. Dust with 1 tablespoon cocoa powder.

In a large saucepan over low heat, warm the 3 sticks butter, the 1 1/2 cups cocoa powder, the coffee, and sugars. Cook until the butter and sugars are melted and the mixture is uniform, whisking occasionally. Remove from the heat and cool to room temperature.

In a large mixing bowl, sift together the flour, baking soda, and salt. In a medium mixing bowl, whisk the eggs and vanilla together. Whisk the egg mixture into the chocolate mixture until combined. Add the wet chocolate mixture into the flour mixture and whisk to combine.

PEANUT BUTTER ICING

1 cup powdered sugar, sifted

½ cup salted chunky peanut butter

½ cup (4 ounces) mascarpone cheese

1 teaspoon vanilla extract

½ teaspoon fine sea salt

CARAMEL SAUCE

1 cup heavy (whipping) cream

1 cup granulated sugar

½ teaspoon fine sea salt

Pour the batter into the prepared pan and bake for 35 minutes, or until a toothpick comes out clean when inserted into the center of the cake. Allow to cool for 30 minutes, then invert onto a cooling rack until the cake comes to room temperature.

MAKE THE PEANUT BUTTER ICING: In the bowl of an electric stand mixer fitted with the paddle attachment, beat together the powdered sugar, peanut butter, mascarpone, vanilla, and salt at medium speed until the mixture is uniform in color and fluffy in texture. Set aside. (You can prepare this ahead and refrigerate for up to 3 days before using. Allow the icing to come to room temperature before filling the sandwiches.)

CREATE THE CARAMEL SAUCE: Heat the cream in a small saucepan to a simmer. When simmering, cover the pan and remove from the heat. In a heavy-bottomed medium pot, combine the sugar and ⅓ cup water. Cook over medium heat without stirring until the sugar is dissolved, the mixture has gone from a rapid bubble to a slower bubble, and a deep amber color is created, about 10 minutes. Do not stir as this will crystallize the sugar. Pour in the warmed cream and add the salt—the caramel will bubble up vigorously, but continue to whisk for about 2 minutes as it cooks more. The sugar may form lumps at the bottom of your pot; this is fine. Continue to whisk vigorously until most of the lumps dissolve, 5 to 8 minutes. The mixture will thicken slightly. Pour through a fine-mesh sieve into a heatproof container, cover, and refrigerate until ready to use. (The caramel will become twice as thick in the fridge. Store any extra in a jar in the fridge for up to 1 week; it's delicious on ice cream.)

ASSEMBLE THE CAKE: Cut off all the edges and the domed top from the cake so that it's level. Split the cake horizontally. Cut the cake into thirds crosswise. You'll be left with six 4-inch squares. Split each square in half and spread about 1 heaping tablespoon of peanut butter frosting on one side and the same amount of caramel sauce on the other. Sandwich the two sides together and cut on a diagonal. Wrap in wax paper or parchment with baker's twine for the full sandwich effect. Store at room temperature until ready to serve.

After a few rounds of struggling to figure out this handsome tart I read about in an old British cookbook given to me by my mother-in-law, I called upon an expert—Roxanne Rosensteel to the rescue! Roxanne is a young pastry chef in Santa Barbara, bursting with creativity and problem-solving acumen. She helped me twist and turn the vague description of a delicious-sounding dessert into a real-life favorite recipe. Her ideas for adding fresh fruit flavors resulted in a lemony bomb—an easy, quick-setting lemon curd topped with bright strawberries and whipped cream. It's simply out-of-this-world delicious. The time it takes to make all of the elements is so worth the effort—but no worries, it can be made in advance and finished with the cream and sliced berries when serving. Its presentation is luscious, unfussy, and casually elegant. I'm already planning my next gathering with this tart as the star guest.

LEMON-STRAWBERRY TART

SERVES 8

CRUST

1½ cups amaretti cookie crumbs

1 stick (4 ounces) unsalted butter, melted

1 tablespoon sugar

¼ teaspoon fine sea salt

FILLING

1 can (14 ounces) sweetened condensed milk

4 egg yolks

2 teaspoons grated lemon zest

½ cup fresh lemon juice (about 5 lemons)

TOPPING

1 cup heavy (whipping) cream

¼ cup sour cream

½ cup sugar

1 teaspoon vanilla extract

2 cups thinly sliced strawberries, for garnish

MAKE THE CRUST: Preheat the oven to 375°F. Lightly grease a 9-inch tart pan.

In a large bowl, stir together the cookie crumbs, melted butter, sugar, and salt. Press the cookie mixture firmly into the tart pan. Bake for 7 minutes and cool on a wire rack. Leave the oven on but reduce the temperature to 325°F.

MAKE THE FILLING: In a large bowl, whisk together the condensed milk, egg yolks, lemon zest, and lemon juice until combined. Pour the lemon mixture into the tart crust and bake for 15 minutes, or until the filling is firm when moved slightly. Let cool on a wire rack, then refrigerate for at least 4 hours or overnight.

PREPARE THE TOPPING: In the bowl of an electric stand mixer fitted with the whisk attachment, whip the heavy cream, sour cream, sugar, and vanilla until soft peaks form. Spread the whipped cream on top of the tart. Top with strawberry slices and serve immediately.

MANGO SEMIFREDDO WITH RASPBERRIES & PISTACHIOS

SERVES 8 TO 10

2 cups roughly chopped mango

2 tablespoons lemon juice

¼ teaspoon ground turmeric

2 cups raspberries

¾ cup sugar

1 tablespoon Cointreau

3 large eggs

2 large egg yolks

½ cup honey

1 teaspoon vanilla extract

2 cups heavy (whipping) cream

⅔ cup roughly chopped pistachios

8 to 10 ladyfingers

"I know it was you, Fredo. You broke my heart. You broke my heart!" I like to quote Michael Corleone from *The Godfather: Part II* whenever I serve the beautiful, luxuriously creamy Italian dessert, semifreddo, even if this dessert doesn't represent familial betrayal to me. If an iconic name matches a dessert, you can bet I'm trying my hand at it. This idea led me to attempting Napoleons once—a million pounds of failed puff pastry and I was done. Not so with this semifreddo.

A semifreddo is a type of "half frozen" dessert from Italy. It's a combination of a mousse-like cream, flavored with fruit, coffee, or booze and layered with cookies of some sort. The whole thing gets frozen and served in slices, and it's a great alternative to an ice cream cake, or a great work-around treat if you're like me and don't have an ice cream machine but still want to make a frozen bomb of a dessert with a lot of wow factor. This one is for big parties, and it's the stuff that even the most major of fictional *mafiosi* might dream about.

In a blender, puree the mango with the lemon juice and turmeric until smooth. Set aside.

In a small saucepan, combine the raspberries with ¼ cup of the sugar, the Cointreau, and 1 tablespoon water and cook over medium heat until the fruit is just beginning to break down and is bubbling, 3 to 5 minutes. Push the raspberry mixture through a fine-mesh sieve into a small bowl (discard the seeds). Refrigerate the puree until ready to assemble.

In a medium metal bowl set over (not in) a pot of simmering water, vigorously whisk together the whole eggs, egg yolks, honey, vanilla, and the remaining ½ cup sugar until you have a pale, thickened mixture that looks like a softly whipped cream, about 6 minutes. (It will look like just eggs for about 4 minutes,

(continued)

then completely transform at minute 5 into a creamy looking pudding.) Cool the egg mixture in the fridge for about 1 hour.

Just before assembling, line a 9 x 5-inch loaf pan with 2 pieces of parchment, one going lengthwise and one crosswise, trimmed to just fit inside the pan but with a 1-inch overhang on the sides for easy removal of the semifreddo upon serving.

In the bowl of an electric stand mixer fitted with the whisk attachment, whip the cream to stiff peaks. Set aside 1 cup of the whipped cream in a small bowl. Fold the mango puree into the remaining whipped cream. Gently fold the chilled egg mixture into the mango cream until just combined.

Scatter ⅓ cup of the chopped pistachios into the lined loaf pan. Pour about half the mango cream on top of the pistachios. Dip each ladyfinger into a generous amount of raspberry puree, careful to thoroughly cover the cookie. Carefully place the cookie lengthwise across the mango cream, making 2 rows of 4 cookies across the pan. Gently spoon any remaining raspberry puree over the ladyfingers once they're all in place. Spoon the reserved whipped cream over the entire surface of the raspberry-coated ladyfingers, smoothing it into as uniform a layer as possible, carefully not integrating it too much into the raspberry layer. Finally, pour the remaining half of the mango cream on top of the whipped cream layer. Smooth the surface with an offset spatula or butter knife. Cover the pan tightly with plastic wrap and freeze for at least 8 hours or overnight.

When ready to serve, remove the plastic wrap, lift the semifreddo out, and set it onto a pretty platter; discard all the parchment paper. Sprinkle the remaining ⅓ cup pistachios over the top of the unmolded semifreddo. Let rest for 10 minutes before serving. Gather a sharp knife, a glass of hot water, and a clean kitchen towel for slicing. In between each slice, dip the knife into the hot water and wipe it with the towel before slicing, to create clean edges and highly visible layers.

Just the name "Eton mess" is enough to provoke my curiosity—a dessert that's *supposed* to be messy, imperfect, and crazy? Sign me up. As a kid, my parents used to joke that the laws of gravity didn't apply to my room. I have since reformed my ways (well, I'm trying anyway!), but I'm immediately drawn to anything resembling the chaos and nuttiness of my natural-born disorganization.

This is a treat born out of chaos—part of a range of British desserts involving meringue, whipped cream, and fruit; the name hails from the famous boys' school in Eton, England. Legend has it the lads would create their own concoctions after their annual cricket match with a rival school. They'd swirl together these disparate, delicious elements into a tumultuous delight. Genius, boys! The resulting dessert is vivid in its taste and irreverence. My interpretation is a departure from the original tower of plain meringue, sweetened whipped cream, and fruit. Mine includes barely sweetened rosé curd and chamomile-infused cream—both tastes accent the sweet raspberry meringue splendidly. Fresh raspberries and extra flowers add pops of texture and fresh flavor. Best of all, the elements can be made in advance, then assembled in a variety of ways, on small plates or crushed together in pretty glasses.

ETON MESS WITH RASPBERRY, CHAMOMILE & ROSÉ CURD

SERVES 6 TO 8

MERINGUES

4 large egg whites (see Note, page 157)

1¼ cups sugar

½ cup dehydrated raspberries, finely ground

½ teaspoon vanilla extract

Pinch of fine sea salt

ROSÉ CURD

4 egg yolks

¼ cup rosé wine

2 tablespoons sugar

MAKE THE MERINGUES: Preheat the oven to 300°F. Line 2 baking sheets with parchment paper.

In the bowl of an electric stand mixer fitted with the whisk attachment, beat the egg whites until soft peaks are formed. Gradually add the sugar, ¼ cup at a time, beating on medium-high speed until the egg whites are glossy and the sugar is dissolved. Add the dehydrated raspberries, vanilla, and salt and beat for another 5 to 10 seconds. Using 2 spoons (1 for scooping, the other for scraping) form 8 to 10 blobs, about 4 inches in

(continued)

CHAMOMILE CREAM

2 cups heavy (whipping) cream

2 heaping tablespoons loose-leaf chamomile tea

1 tablespoon sugar

1 pint fresh raspberries

½ cup fresh chamomile flowers, stems removed

diameter, onto the baking sheets, leaving a little room between each meringue for them to puff up slightly as they bake.

Bake the meringues for 25 to 30 minutes, until golden brown and slightly hollow when you tap them. Turn the oven off and leave the meringues in the oven for about 1 hour or up to 4 hours. Remove from the oven and allow to cool (if you want to do this ahead, place the meringues in a sealed container for up to a day). The meringues will be crunchy on the outside and chewy on the inside.

MAKE THE ROSÉ CURD: In a medium saucepan, combine the egg yolks, wine, and sugar and whisk vigorously over low heat until it goes from thin liquid to thick cream, about 2 minutes. Pour the mixture through a fine-mesh sieve into a bowl. Cover the curd with plastic wrap until ready to serve.

WHIP THE CHAMOMILE CREAM: In a medium saucepan, heat the cream until almost boiling. Stir in the tea, cover the pot, and remove from the heat. Let the cream steep for 20 minutes, then strain the liquid through a fine-mesh sieve into a bowl. Allow the cream to cool in the refrigerator until ready to serve.

In the bowl of an electric stand mixer fitted with the whisk attachment, whip the chilled chamomile cream with the sugar until soft peaks form.

ASSEMBLE THE DESSERT: Place a layer of about 3 meringues on a serving platter or cake stand. Dollop one-third of the chamomile cream onto the meringues, dot with a few fresh raspberries, and top with one-third of the rosé curd. Repeat the process two times, finishing the mountain of meringue and cream with more fresh raspberries and a smattering of fresh chamomile flowers. Serve immediately.

note Make sure your bowl and whisk are very clean before using—just the tiniest hint of water or moisture and your meringues might not set or stiffen. When preparing to deal with those egg whites, take your time to get each egg white completely out of the eggshell with no trace of yolk.

BLUEBERRY GALETTE WITH MASCARPONE & OAT CRUST

MAKES ONE 9-INCH GALETTE

The humble elegance of a fruit galette and the forgiving nature of its free-form shape both add to the reasons that it's one of my go-to desserts. You can riff on any seasonal fruit (stone fruits, figs, and berries are my first choice)—adding intriguing flavors and different textures to the magic synthesis of bubbling fruit, a bit of sugar, and butter. In this version, oat flour complements blueberry's juicy tones just brilliantly. The mascarpone is my decadent secret weapon: It's a subtle flavor, but it prevents the fruit juices from penetrating the bottom layer of the crust, and it adds a touch of creamy richness to the entire dessert. With a heaping scoop of ice cream at a party, or unadorned as a perfect picnic treat, this galette always hits the spot.

CRUST

½ cup oat flour

¾ cup all-purpose flour, plus more for the rolling pin (see Notes, page 160)

1 heaping tablespoon granulated sugar

¼ teaspoon fine sea salt

1 stick (4 ounces) cold unsalted butter, cut into ½-inch cubes

3 to 5 tablespoons ice-cold water

1 large egg yolk, beaten

FILLING

⅔ cup (8 ounces) mascarpone cheese

2 teaspoons honey

3 cups fresh or frozen blueberries

2 teaspoons cornstarch

3 tablespoons granulated sugar

¼ teaspoon grated lemon zest

Pinch of fine sea salt

1 large egg

2 tablespoons turbinado sugar

START THE CRUST: In a food processor, combine both flours, the granulated sugar, and salt and pulse a few times to just combine. Pulse the butter into the flour mixture in several short bursts until the mixture resembles large peas, about 10 seconds. Add 3 tablespoons of the ice water, a tablespoon at a time, pulsing for about 2 seconds after each addition. Add the egg yolk and pulse just until the dough is formed (you may need to add a tablespoon or more water to form a mass). Squeeze the dough into a disk, cover tightly in plastic wrap, and refrigerate for at least 1 hour.

MAKE THE FILLING: In the bowl of an electric stand mixer fitted with the whisk attachment, whisk together the mascarpone and honey until combined. Set aside. In a large bowl, toss together the blueberries, cornstarch, granulated sugar, lemon zest, and salt.

PREPARE THE GALETTE: Line a baking sheet with parchment. Remove the dough from the refrigerator and soften the disk by giving it a few whacks with the back of a rolling pin. Roll the dough out with a floured rolling pin on the lined baking sheet, working quickly to ensure a light, flaky crust, until you have a

(continued)

12-inch round of dough. Spread the mascarpone mixture onto the surface of the dough, leaving a 2-inch border around the perimeter. Top with the blueberry mixture, again leaving 2 inches uncovered. Pull the 2-inch border of dough up and over the blueberries, leaving the edges of the dough rustic or trimming them if a cleaner edge is desired. Refrigerate the galette for at least 15 minutes and up to 1 hour (this will keep the crust edges cleaner and the dough crispy after baking). Preheat the oven to 400°F.

Remove the galette from the fridge. In a small bowl, beat the whole egg with 1 tablespoon water. Brush the edges of the galette generously with the egg wash and dust with the turbinado sugar.

Bake for 30 minutes, then reduce the oven temperature to 375°F and rotate the baking sheet front to back for even baking. Bake for 20 to 25 minutes, until the crust is a deep golden brown (see Notes).

Allow the galette to fully cool on the pan for at least 1 hour, after that it can sit on the countertop until ready to serve. It will continue to cook as it cools, making the crust and fruit more solid.

notes

- Occasionally I like to substitute some of the all-purpose flour in a recipe with a less refined grain flour. I play with leaving at least half the flour as is and replacing the other half with spelt, rye, oat, or whole wheat flour.

- When cooking a fruit galette, taste the fruit first: If your fruit is in peak season, juicy, and sweet, reduce the amount of sugar so its natural sweetness will shine through. If you're working with fruit that's a tad flatter in flavor, increase the sugar by a tablespoon or so, or even add some fruit jam or preserves to boost its flavor. I use frozen fruit often with fantastic results, just taste it and adjust accordingly.

- Color in the crust is flavor! Don't be afraid to let the crust become a deep, golden brown (I like mine almost burned); all that caramelization lends a delicious, toasty taste.

Remember the Ben and Jerry's Cherry Garcia ice cream craze of the early '90s? It was my dad's favorite thing to scoop into after one of his elaborate dinners. I considered the flavor "too adult"—all that fruit and dark chocolate disturbing my ice cream soup (better to slurp ice cream down by tipping the bowl to my lips, no spoon required!). Now I'm very intrigued by the tasty add-in combos of the popular ice cream flavors of my childhood, and I am excited to share this no-bake dessert, which is totally rich.

Made primarily with cashews, honey, and a little coconut oil, this freezes into silky, elegant cakes, reminiscent of cheesecake and ice cream. It's amazing what you can spin up in a blender, and while it's not our role as cooks to necessarily fool or trick guests, I do take pleasure in making something that looks downright artery-clogging to my guests, allowing them to "ooh" and "aah" before I reveal that it's made with wholesome ingredients. Shock and awe abound!

MINI CHERRY-CHOCOLATE CAKES

MAKES 12 INDIVIDUAL CAKES

FILLING

2 cups raw cashews

½ cup coconut oil, melted

⅓ cup honey

¼ cup lemon juice

Pinch of fine sea salt

CRUST

4 dates, pitted and roughly chopped

1 cup walnuts

¼ cup unsweetened shredded coconut

2 tablespoons cacao nibs

1 tablespoon olive oil

¼ teaspoon fine sea salt

MAKE THE FILLING: In a medium bowl, combine the cashews with water to cover. Let them soak for at least 4 hours, or overnight, then drain and set aside.

In a high-speed blender or food processor, combine the drained cashews, coconut oil, honey, lemon juice, salt, and ¼ cup water until smooth and creamy. Set the filling aside.

CREATE THE CRUST: In a food processor, combine the dates, walnuts, coconut, cacao nibs, olive oil, and salt and pulse into a coarse meal. Add a little water to the mixture, tablespoon by tablespoon, in order for it to become one crumbly looking mass. Set aside at room temperature.

(continued)

TOPPING

¼ cup cherry jam

1 teaspoon vanilla extract

12 jarred amarena cherries in syrup (I like Toschi, page 9)

MAKE THE TOPPING: In a blender or food processor, combine the cherry jam, vanilla, and 2 tablespoons water and process until smooth. Set the cherry topping aside.

Line 12 cups of a muffin tin with parchment strips, 2 strips in each cup in a crisscross pattern, leaving 4 tabs hanging outside the cup so you can lift the cakes out when they are done.

ASSEMBLE THE CAKES: Firmly pack about 1 tablespoon of the date crust into the bottom of each lined muffin cup. Scoop 1 heaping tablespoon of the cashew filling into each muffin cup, then divide the remaining filling among all the cups. Smear a little jam mixture over the top of each cake. Sprinkle a pinch of the date crust mixture on top of the jam. Place a cherry off center of each cake.

Freeze the cakes for at least 6 hours, or overnight. When ready to serve, remove the muffin tin from the freezer and let it rest at room temperature for 30 minutes. Gingerly wiggle the tabs to pull the cakes out, carefully remove the parchment strips, and serve cherry-side up.

> note This recipe takes a little patience, but it can be made in advance—and it's so good, your efforts won't go unnoticed.

Once, when I was young and foolish, I attempted to make a singular, giant flan for a hundred people, and I didn't realize that the science of baking doesn't allow one to scale up a recipe by just multiplying the ingredients by ten. I stayed up all night babysitting this flan in the oven, terrified that the gigantic beast would not set, and that I was moments away from a mess of scrambled eggs and sugar. By some stroke of kindness at the hands of the flan gods, the entire thing did cook correctly—it just took all night! It's been about twelve years since I've recovered from flan PTSD and I'm so glad to correct my anxiety-inducing recipe with a much easier and even tastier version of the creamy classic. A custard infused with rosewater and topped with a cascade of rose petals—what could be better? This riff is very simple to make ahead and is a real crowd-pleaser for a girls' night.

ROSE FLAN

SERVES 6

1 cup sugar

1½ cups heavy (whipping) cream

1 vanilla bean, halved lengthwise

12 large egg yolks

1 can (14 ounces) sweetened condensed milk

1 teaspoon rosewater

Candied Rose Petals
(page 60)

Preheat the oven to 350°F.

In a medium heavy-bottomed pan, combine the sugar and ¼ cup water and bring to a boil, without stirring, over high heat. Cook without stirring until the sugar is dissolved and has turned a deep amber color, about 10 minutes. Divide the caramel among six 5-ounce ramekins, quickly swirling the bottom of each ramekin so the caramel is as even as possible. Set aside to cool.

Place the cream in a small saucepan. Scrape the vanilla seeds out of the pod into the cream and add the scraped vanilla pod. Bring the cream to a simmer over medium heat. As soon as it simmers, remove from the heat, cover, and allow the vanilla bean to steep for 15 minutes. Discard the vanilla pod and cool the cream in the fridge for about 15 minutes, until it reaches room temperature.

In a large bowl, beat the egg yolks, then whisk in the cooled cream, condensed milk, and rosewater. Strain the liquid through a fine-mesh sieve into the caramel-lined ramekins. Cover each ramekin tightly with foil and place in a 9 x 13-inch pan that is at least 2 inches deep. Pour in warm water around the ramekins until it reaches halfway up the sides of the ramekins.

Bake the flans for 45 to 50 minutes, until they are just set in the center (jiggle them slightly to be sure they're set). Remove the baked flans from the water bath and remove the foil from the ramekins to let them cool. Once the flans are room temperature, refrigerate them for at least 6 to 8 hours to chill.

When ready to serve, run an offset spatula or small knife around the edges of each flan to loosen, dipping your tool in very hot water as necessary to maintain clean edges. Invert each flan onto a plate and scatter a few candied rose petals across the top. Serve immediately.

COCONUT LAMINGTONS

MAKES 16 LAMINGTONS

Rich pound cake enrobed in a generous bath of chocolate ganache? Yes, please! These cheeky petits fours, popular in Australia, are a burst of coconut goodness. There's nothing finer to serve for a small party or even to bring as a hostess gift. My interpretation includes even more coconut flavor, with the addition of coconut milk in the cake batter and large, toasted flakes. When it comes to coconut, I am of the "more is more" school of thought. Perhaps it's my mother's Southern roots, where coconut cream pies, triple layer cakes, and coconut macaroons dominated the dessert table.

½ cup vegetable oil, plus more for greasing the pan

1¾ cups all-purpose flour, plus more for flouring the pan

¾ cup sugar

2 teaspoons vanilla extract

2 large eggs

1 cup coconut milk

1¾ teaspoons baking powder

¾ teaspoon fine sea salt

3 cups unsweetened large coconut flakes

2 bittersweet chocolate bars (4 ounces each), broken into 1-inch pieces

½ cup whole milk

Preheat the oven to 350°F. Lightly grease and flour an 8 x 8-inch baking pan.

In a medium bowl, whisk together the vegetable oil, sugar, vanilla, eggs, and coconut milk. In a large bowl, sift together the flour, baking powder, and salt. Add the milk mixture all at once into the flour mixture and mix until just combined. Spoon the batter into the baking pan and smooth the surface with a spatula (the batter will be quite thick).

Bake the cake for 35 minutes, or until golden brown and a toothpick inserted in the center comes out clean. Cool in the pan for 10 minutes, then invert the cake onto a wire rack to cool completely.

In a large skillet, lightly toast the coconut flakes over medium-low heat until they turn golden and become aromatic, about 3 minutes. Transfer the golden coconut flakes to a baking sheet to cool.

Place the chocolate in a microwave-safe bowl and microwave in 10-second bursts, stirring between each, until melted (or you can melt it in a double boiler). Whisk in the milk until combined.

Cut the cake into 2-inch squares. Using a fork, dip into the chocolate mixture to coat completely, and roll in the toasted coconut. Let set on a wire rack for about 1 hour before serving.

Just seeing the word *falooda* on a menu in Panaji, India, was enough to make me order it. . . . I had no idea that I was in for the wackiest, sweetest, and most refreshing dessert drink I've ever experienced. It looks like a bubble tea gone crazy! I discovered I could get one at most cafés all over India, and so everywhere I went, my little-girl dreams came true with each spoonful of this pink madness.

My interpretation is a very distant cousin of the traditional treat, with the addition of fresh pineapple and items you can get at any American grocery; it's also a little less sticky sweet. This whimsical dessert is flexible to your personal taste and mood. The basic formula is a blob of ice cream, a little sweetener (in India and Pakistan, they often use rose syrup), a dash of milk, chopped cooked rice noodles, a gelatinous item (such as tapioca, chia, or basil seed), then whipped cream to take it completely over the top.

THINK PINK FALOODAS

SERVES 4

½ cup small pearl tapioca

1 cup dry rice noodles (about 2 ounces)

½ cup heavy (whipping) cream

½ teaspoon rosewater

1 cup whole milk

1⅓ cups canned or fresh diced pineapple

1 pint orange sherbet

4 teaspoons grenadine

Rainbow sprinkles, for garnish

In a medium saucepan, combine the tapioca pearls and 4 cups water and bring to a boil. Cook over medium heat until the pearls have softened, about 15 minutes. Rinse under cold water, drain, and set aside.

Bring 2 cups water to a boil. Place the dried noodles in a heat-proof medium bowl and pour the boiling water over the top. Let the noodles soften for 1 to 2 minutes. Rinse under cold water and drain. Roughly chop the noodles into inch-long pieces and set aside. In a medium bowl, with an electric mixer, whip the cream until soft peaks form. Stir the rosewater into the whole milk.

In each of 4 pretty drinking glasses, layer the ingredients in this order: ¼ cup chopped noodles, ⅓ cup pineapple, ¼ cup tapioca pearls, and 1 scoop orange sherbet. Pour ¼ cup of rosewater flavored milk over everything and top with 1 teaspoon grenadine. Garnish each glass with whipped cream and sprinkles. Serve each falooda with a straw and a spoon—the fun of this drink is stirring up the dessert yourself and blending the colors and textures together in each bite.

I've worked with ice cream for the past five years, mainly taking photographs for the fabulous Portland ice cream shop Salt & Straw. As an accidental ice cream–ologist (childhood dreams do come true!), I've learned my way around the wackiest flavors and most challenging styling conditions. ("It's MELTING, oh my God, it's REALLY melting!" says David, my food stylist. "Okay, I'm shooting shooting shooting, get ready with another scoop, NOW!" I say.) But what I've discovered is that truly special ice cream deserves an equally wild, inventive cone, one you can recklessly doctor up with your favorite candies and sprinkles. Enter the elusive unicone, a mythical creature that can be made in any kitchen and brings sparkle to any and all gatherings. Kids and adults alike deserve epicurean magic.

UNICONES

MAKES 10 CONES

2 dark chocolate bars (4 ounces each), cut into pieces

½ cup sprinkles

½ cup dried edible untreated rose petals or Candied Rose Petals (page 60)

½ cup crushed M&M's

½ cup nonpareils

10 ice cream sugar cones

Place the chocolate in a microwave-safe bowl and microwave in 10-second bursts, stirring between each, until melted (or you can melt it in a double boiler).

Line a baking sheet with parchment paper. Set out all the toppings (sprinkles, rose petals, M&M's, and nonpareils) in small bowls.

Dip the top two inches of a cone into the melted chocolate, then roll the chocolate side in each small bowl of topping or sprinkle a little bit of all the toppings onto the wet chocolate. Work quickly as things can get messy and drippy. Place the finished cones on the baking sheet, open side down, and let dry. If working on a hot day, place the baking sheet in the refrigerator to set.

SPICED PUMPKIN PARFAITS

MAKES 6 TO 8 PARFAITS

Who can resist a chilled mess of pumpkin goodness, topped off with whipped cream and crushed gingersnaps? Everyone is powerless against this autumnal siren of a dessert—I've never seen it last more than five minutes at a table with my friends. Inspired by my dad's famous pumpkin chiffon pie, I deconstructed and rebuilt it in layered form with a few modifications: less sugar, more punchy gingersnaps (store-bought is absolutely fine!), and a dusting of candied ginger. Sometimes all I want at holidays are traditional desserts; other times I throw caution to the wind and dart out in new directions, and these parfaits were the lucky strike on one such wily occasion!

CREAM

1 cup heavy (whipping) cream

⅓ cup plain whole-milk Greek yogurt

2 tablespoons powdered sugar

Pinch of fine sea salt

CUSTARD

2 teaspoons unflavored gelatin

¼ cup Cointreau

1½ cups canned unsweetened pumpkin puree

½ cup heavy (whipping) cream

½ cup plus 2 tablespoons granulated sugar

3 large egg yolks

¾ teaspoon ground cinnamon

½ teaspoon ground ginger

¼ teaspoon freshly grated nutmeg

¼ teaspoon ground allspice

¼ teaspoon fine sea salt

4 pasteurized large egg whites

MAKE THE CREAM: In the bowl of an electric stand mixer fitted with the whisk attachment, whip the cream, Greek yogurt, powdered sugar, and salt until stiff peaks form. Transfer to another bowl and refrigerate until ready to assemble.

MAKE THE CUSTARD: In a small heatproof bowl, whisk together the gelatin and Cointreau and set over a bowl of warm water, for about 2 minutes, until the gelatin has dissolved. Leave in the warm water bowl while the other ingredients are prepared.

In a medium saucepan, whisk together the pumpkin, cream, ½ cup of the granulated sugar, the egg yolks, cinnamon, ground ginger, nutmeg, allspice, and salt until incorporated. Stir the mixture with a wooden spoon over medium heat for 10 minutes. Remove from the heat, pour into a glass or metal bowl, whisk in the gelatin mixture, and refrigerate to cool.

In the bowl of an electric stand mixer fitted with the whisk attachment, whisk the egg whites and the remaining 2 tablespoons granulated sugar until stiff peaks form. Fold the egg whites into the chilled pumpkin mixture until uniform.

2 cups roughly crushed
gingersnap cookies

Freshly grated nutmeg

2 tablespoons finely chopped
candied ginger

ASSEMBLE THE PARFAITS: Gather 6 to 8 cocktail glasses.
Place 2 heaping tablespoons of pumpkin mixture in the bottom
of each glass, top with 1 heaping tablespoon whipped cream
followed by 1 heaping tablespoon crushed cookies. Repeat the
layering once more. Garnish with a little freshly grated nutmeg
and crystallized ginger. Chill in the fridge for at least 4 hours
before serving.

note The coconut cream topping is absolutely decadent—manna from the gods—and creates a gimme-more dessert.

CHILI-LIME PINEAPPLE WITH COCONUT CREAM

SERVES 4

1 can (14 ounces) whole-fat coconut milk

1 medium pineapple

¼ cup coconut oil, melted

¼ cup packed light brown sugar

1 teaspoon chili powder

Fine sea salt

Grated zest of 1 lime, reserving about ½ teaspoon for garnish

2 tablespoons honey (or more to taste)

1 teaspoon vanilla extract

½ cup unsweetened coconut flakes, toasted, for garnish (optional)

Pineapple for dessert can be better than chocolate—I realize this is a bold statement! But it's one of the many surprising truths I learned while traveling in Vietnam and India. With a ripe pineapple, it's possible to bite into a slice of honey-sweet, fragrant fruit and be bowled over by the heady romance and tropical grandeur it brings to mind.

Refrigerate the coconut milk in its can overnight, or for at least 6 hours, to allow the fat solids to rise to the top and the remaining water to settle in the bottom of the can.

Preheat the oven to 450°F. Line a baking sheet with parchment paper. (If you have a large pineapple, you may need 2 baking sheets.)

Peel the pineapple and cut it crosswise into eight ½-inch-thick slices (leaving the core is fine, as the cooking will soften it). Rub each slice of pineapple with a little coconut oil. Arrange the slices on the prepared baking sheet in an even layer without much overlapping. Sprinkle both sides of the pineapple disks with the brown sugar, chili powder, and a pinch of salt.

Bake for 20 minutes, flipping the slices after 10 minutes. Remove from the oven and let cool to room temperature. Sprinkle with the lime zest.

When ready to serve, open the can of coconut milk and scoop the solid coconut mass that has risen to the top into the bowl of an electric stand mixer fitted with the whisk attachment (you can use the coconut water at the bottom of the can for smoothies or just for drinking). Add the honey, vanilla, and a pinch of salt to the bowl. Whisk on high speed until you have a smooth, uniform mixture that resembles traditional whipped cream, about 5 minutes.

For each portion, plate a pineapple slice and add a dollop of coconut cream. Garnish with a pinch of lime zest and coconut flakes, if desired.

Remember Sour Patch Kids and their gooey chewiness? This nubby, texture-filled pudding is a throwback to the core essence of those candies—that eating is supposed to be just totally FUN sometimes. Tapioca pudding, dressed up with natural fruit, sesame seeds, and coconut milk, is the dessert to pull out when your girlfriends are coming over to watch cheesy '80s romance movies.

This version uses coconut as the milk base and is backed up by a touch of spice from the cardamom and ginger. The roasted nectarines playfully elevate the pudding, and the resulting richness is a little bit sweet and sour, but you can use whatever fruit is in season. I like to roast stone fruit to concentrate their natural sweetness, but if you have perfect room temperature fruit such as banana, figs, or strawberries, by all means dice that up and put it on top—you cannot go wrong here.

COCONUT TAPIOCA PUDDING WITH ROASTED NECTARINES

SERVES 6

½ cup small tapioca pearls

2 cups coconut milk

½ teaspoon fine sea salt

⅓ cup granulated sugar

2 large eggs

½ teaspoon coconut extract

½ teaspoon vanilla extract

¼ teaspoon ground cardamom

¼ teaspoon ground ginger

2 medium nectarines, roughly chopped

1 tablespoon light brown sugar

1 tablespoon smoked sesame seeds

In a medium saucepan, combine the tapioca, coconut milk, 1 cup water, and ¼ teaspoon of the salt and bring to a boil, stirring constantly. Reduce the heat to low and simmer for 5 minutes, stirring and adding the granulated sugar gradually, until the sugar is dissolved.

In a medium bowl, beat the eggs. Add ¼ cup of the hot tapioca mixture to the beaten eggs, whisking to combine. Whisk the egg/tapioca mixture back into the pan, and bring the mixture back to a boil, whisking constantly to avoid curdling. Stir in the coconut extract, vanilla, cardamom, and ginger. When the mixture boils, reduce the heat to low and simmer, whisking, until the tapioca pearls are cooked through but still have some tooth to them, about 9 minutes. Pour into a container, let cool to room temperature, seal with a lid or plastic wrap, and refrigerate for at least 4 hours. (The pudding will thicken significantly after about 4 hours in the refrigerator.)

Preheat the oven to 400°F. Line a baking sheet with parchment paper.

In a medium bowl, toss together the chopped nectarines, brown sugar, and remaining ¼ teaspoon salt. Scatter the fruit onto the baking sheet and roast for about 10 minutes, a little longer if you want your fruit very soft, a little shorter to retain texture.

When ready to serve, whisk 4 to 6 tablespoons of water into the pudding to lighten it (it gets quite thick in the fridge). Divide the pudding among 6 pretty glasses. Top each glass with ¼ cup roasted nectarines and a pinch of smoked sesame seeds.

TINY TAKEAWAYS

get carried away

I love sending guests home with a little extra treat or bringing hosts a homemade thank-you—something for them to store away in the pantry, fridge, or lunch box for those days that need a boost or those ordinary dishes that you want to make extra lovely. With a little creative forethought and effort, it's possible to make each eating experience sparkle. I learned this gesture from my parents who always brought something to friends from their garden or kitchen—even something as casual as a jar of homemade salad dressing or a small plate of brownies from a new recipe they'd been experimenting with.

This concept of cooking a tiny something extra was demonstrated beautifully in another generous fashion by my friend Adrian Hale in Portland, who often hosted my husband and me for lively dinner parties. When the night was done and we bundled ourselves up at her door, she would surprise us with an unassuming platter of muffins "to take home; you can have them for breakfast." In doing so, Adrian sent the spirit of the cozy evening home with us: We felt lucky enough to wake up to her baked goods after feasting with her the night before. This little act of kindness and care was like being wrapped up in the happiest, warmest blanket in the world—and made her dinner party even more unforgettable.

With a bit of work and planning, we all have the power to make our friends and family feel extra special and taken care of. It can be as simple as a jar of homemade Four-Seed Granola with Dried Cherries (page 182)—double the batch and save some for yourself—some Homemade Popcorn, Three Ways (page 194), Spice Blend Chai (page 193), or Scotch Caramels with Smoked Salt (page 186). These are simple gestures that create a lasting, happy impression.

presenting treats to give

I like to have a few items on hand that give edible gifts the extra polish. These are all inexpensive, easy to find, and add a little sparkle to your recipient's day.

- Parchment paper—easy to find in either an untreated natural brown color or plain white, makes a great catchall for quickly wrapping up a few mochis or shaping into a cone for homemade popcorn.

- Wax paper—similar to parchment, but with a slight translucence, making it the perfect thing to wrap homemade candies in, such as Scotch Caramels with Smoked Salt (page 186). It's available at any grocery store.

- Wrapping paper—I like to save pretty wrapping or craft paper and cut it into large strips to tape over any gift already wrapped in parchment or wax paper.

- Washi tape—having a few brightly colored tapes makes labeling and sealing gifts a cinch; just write the name of your sweet treat directly onto the tape. Available at many design shops or paper-goods stores.

- Weck jars—inexpensive, chic canning jars that come in a range of sizes with rubber tops, little metal clamps, and a strawberry mark imprinted on nice glass. They are sold at design shops, home goods stores, as well as many hardware stores, and make the perfect vessel for Labneh Balls (page 202), Four-Seed Granola with Dried Cherries (page 182), or Kale Pesto (page 201).

- Old jam jars—I save all the jam and jelly jars we go through in a big box in our closet for impromptu gift giving. I like the French Bonne Maman jars with their cute red-and-white-checked lid the best.

- Tea towels—I have a stack of inexpensive tea towels, mostly purchased from IKEA and other big box stores. They make an excellent wrapping for Irish soda bread or a batch of cookies. And your giftee can reuse the cloth in her own kitchen.

FOUR-SEED GRANOLA WITH DRIED CHERRIES

MAKES ABOUT 6 CUPS

Having a good granola recipe up your sleeve is a great party trick. It's flexible and easily adjusted, depending on the state of your mood and pantry and what's piquing your interest at the market. It always tastes good as breakfast or as a late-afternoon snack, but I eat it most often just from a tiny, pretty bowl with my fingers. Granola also makes a perfect hostess gift when packed into a little jar or tucked into a cute bag.

3 cups rolled oats

½ cup puffed quinoa

¼ cup sesame seeds or flaxseeds or a mixture of the two

¼ cup pumpkin seeds

¼ cup sunflower seeds

1 teaspoon fine sea salt

1 teaspoon ground cinnamon

½ teaspoon freshly grated nutmeg

½ cup olive oil

½ cup maple syrup

1 teaspoon vanilla extract

1 cup roasted whole hazelnuts

1 cup dried cherries

Preheat the oven to 350°F. Line a rimmed baking sheet with parchment paper or a silicone baking mat.

In a large bowl, mix the oats, puffed quinoa, sesame or flaxseeds, pumpkin seeds, sunflower seeds, salt, cinnamon, and nutmeg until thoroughly mixed together.

In a separate bowl, whisk together the olive oil, maple syrup, and vanilla. Combine the seed mixture with the wet ingredients and mix until everything is sticky and moistened. Spread the granola on the prepared baking sheet, gently pressing down to create an even layer. Cook the granola for 30 minutes, stirring every 10 minutes to make sure everything browns evenly, until the granola has slightly hardened and is a toasty brown color. Remove the granola and allow it to cool and set completely. Once cool, transfer the granola to a large bowl and stir in the hazelnuts and dried cherries.

Store in small or large airtight containers, such as canning jars. It will keep for about 1 month in the pantry.

Mochi are a range of Japanese desserts made mostly from rice flour and sugar. Many other countries have appropriated and altered these gelatinous, lightly sweet little desserts—in Taiwan, mochi cakes are served in small squares as a topping for flavored shaved ice or atop a bubble tea; in Hawaii, coconut milk is added for richness. This version is so easy to make, no more fuss than a basic quick bread, and the results are so pretty! The best part is these mochi are naturally gluten-free and vegan, making them a lovely hostess gift or party favor, inclusive of all eaters. They make a great teatime snack and are a favorite light nibble at a picnic lunch. The mellow, slightly bitter flavor of matcha tea offsets the sweetness.

MATCHA MOCHI

MAKES ABOUT 45 MOCHI

Coconut oil, for greasing the pan

3 cups sweet rice flour (see Note)

2 cups sugar

2 tablespoons matcha powder, plus a little extra for dusting

1 teaspoon baking powder

Pinch of fine sea salt

1½ cups coconut milk

1 teaspoon vanilla extract

Cornstarch, for dusting

Preheat the oven to 325°F. Grease a 9 x 13-inch pan liberally with coconut oil.

In a large bowl, mix together the sweet rice flour, sugar, matcha powder, baking powder, and salt. In a separate bowl, whisk together the coconut milk, vanilla, and 2 cups water. Pour the milk mixture into the flour mixture and whisk to combine.

Pour the mochi batter into the prepared pan, cover with foil, and bake for 50 minutes. Let cool uncovered for at least 2 hours. Invert onto a cutting board dusted with cornstarch and a little matcha. Cut lengthwise into 5 strips and then into nine 1½-inch squares. Clean the knife in between cuts for even edges. Dust all sides of the squares lightly in cornstarch to prevent sticking. The mochi will keep in a covered container for about 3 days at room temperature.

note It's critical to purchase sweet rice flour for this recipe, not the more commonly found brown rice or rice flour. Sweet rice flour is made from glutinous, sticky rice and it is what gives the mochi body and chew. It's available to buy through Bob's Red Mill, Asian groceries, or online. I like Mochiko brand best.

SCOTCH CARAMELS WITH SMOKED SALT

MAKES 4 DOZEN 1½-INCH
CARAMELS

Once the coziness of winter descends upon us, I like to get cracking on candy making. A bite of luscious caramel is a nice way to end the day, a party—or in this case, a cookbook. Rest assured, caramels are not that difficult to make. Adding a splash of single-malt Scotch (always a luxury, but an especially sophisticated touch here) and a smattering of smoked salt takes these buttery bobs to the next level.

---

4 tablespoons unsalted butter, plus more for greasing the pan

1 cup heavy (whipping) cream

½ teaspoon fine sea salt

1 cup granulated sugar

½ cup packed light brown sugar

¼ cup light corn syrup

1 teaspoon Scotch whisky

Smoked sea salt, for garnish

Line an 8 x 8-inch baking pan with parchment paper, letting some hang over the sides. (You can also use foil, but parchment will give it a smoother bottom.) Grease the lined pan with cooking spray or butter. Transfer the prepared pan to the refrigerator.

In a small saucepan, combine the cream, butter, and fine sea salt and bring to a simmer. Remove from the heat and set aside.

In a medium saucepan, combine both sugars, corn syrup, and ¼ cup water and bring to a boil. Gently swirl the pan until the sugar dissolves, and keep swirling until the sugar becomes a pale golden caramel, about 8 minutes, or until a candy thermometer registers 320°F. (Keep a pastry brush and water handy to wipe the sides of the pan in case sugar crystals form.)

Carefully whisk the cream mixture into the hot caramel—it will bubble robustly and triple in volume. Simmer the liquid, stirring often, until the mixture reaches 240°F on a candy thermometer, about 9 minutes. (If you want to check its doneness, take a small drop of the mixture and put it in cold water. It should form a ball that is firm but still flexible.) Quickly stir in the Scotch.

Remove the prepared pan from the fridge and pour the hot caramel onto the lined surface, smoothing it evenly—it should set immediately. Sprinkle the surface with a little sea salt. Let it rest for at least 2 hours at room temperature to firm up.

Remove the caramels from the pan and cut them into rectangles. Butter the knife in between cuts for clean edges. If you'd like, you can wrap each square in a small piece of wax paper. Store in an airtight container for up to 1 week.

Restraint? I'm not fond of it. This recipe includes all my favorite flavors—bourbon, salt, black pepper, and good-quality dark chocolate—and turns them into a big kid's delight. Remember Magic Shell from your favorite cheapo ice cream shop? That crackly chocolate was amazing; it was SCIENCE happening before our big, hungry eyes.

My husband, who is also my collaborator, and I were recently asked to make a video depicting how to make this sexy stuff for TheKitchn.com. Much to my surprise, it includes only two ingredients: chocolate and coconut oil. The coconut oil turns the chocolate sauce into a solid once it meets with the cold of ice cream. Let's bamboozle adult ice cream lovers even more with spice, crunchy salt, and booze. Yeah, baby! There's only one thing more magical than original magic—and that's whiskey magic. Oh, the joys of grown-up treats.

WHISKEY-PEPPER MAGIC SHELL

SERVES 6 TO 8

2 cups (about 7 ounces) dark chocolate pieces

½ cup coconut oil

2 tablespoons plus 1 teaspoon of your favorite bourbon or rye

½ teaspoon crunchy sea salt (such as Celtic Sea Salt, sel gris, or fleur de sel)

½ teaspoon freshly ground black pepper

½ teaspoon ground cloves

Ice cream, for serving

In a medium heavy-bottomed saucepan, melt the chocolate and coconut oil over medium heat. Stir in the bourbon, salt, and spices. Stir constantly until everything is melted and combined, then remove from the heat. If using right away, keep warm until you've scooped out your ice cream. If saving for a future dessert, pour the sauce into a sealable container and refrigerate for up to 1 week and then gently reheat before using.

When ready to serve, scoop your favorite ice cream (coffee, caramel, and vanilla are all great) and pour about ¼ cup warm sauce over the scoop. Allow 20 seconds for the shell to form—you can repeat if desired for a double-thick shell.

CHOCOLATE-TAHINI BUTTER

MAKES 1½ CUPS

1/2 cup unsweetened cocoa powder

1/2 cup honey

Pinch of fine sea salt

1 teaspoon vanilla extract

1 cup roasted tahini

I'm as guilty as the next gal of getting immersed in my work and hardly pausing for lunch. When I'm working on a big project, I get in the habit of just grabbing the peanut butter jar and slathering it on a hearty piece of bread before trudging on. Nowadays I'm making an effort to prepare meals and snacks in advance, and all that is grand, but it's helpful to have a bit of delicious convenience for the desperate times when my old nut butter and toast combo is all I can manage. Hello, chocolate-tahini butter, a fantastic upgrade to my go-to snack! The cocoa powder adds a depth and gentle sweetness to the earthy, understated flavor of the sesame-based tahini. With a dash of honey and touch of salt, this stuff is so, so good, even right out of the jar on a spoon. Also, this butter takes the Sweet Tahini Buns (page 49) to a whole new level.

In a medium bowl, mix together the cocoa powder and 1/2 cup very hot water, stirring until it makes a smooth paste. Add the honey, salt, and vanilla and stir to combine. When the honey is well incorporated, stir in the tahini paste until completely combined. (You might need to add a few more tablespoons of hot water to thin the mixture to the right consistency. Add 1 tablespoon at a time and stir to check consistency. You shouldn't have to add more than 3 tablespoons to get the right texture.) Let the butter rest for at least an hour before serving, to allow the flavors to mingle and brighten.

If you wish to give these as gifts, spoon the spread into small canning jars and label. This will keep at room temperature for 3 days, or up to 1 month in the fridge, but you should bring it to room temperature before serving.

In India, the word *chai* just means tea—and can be served countless ways, depending on the region and family tradition, but you can always count on it to soothe the soul. With the general chaos of the city streets, a moment to enjoy a tiny cup of chai is a welcome respite, with its gentle touch of sweetness and spice. This blend includes warming notes from the cardamom, ginger, cloves, and peppercorns, and it is positively sultry when steeped with whole milk and a little sugar.

SPICE BLEND CHAI

MAKES ¾ CUP (ENOUGH FOR 12 CUPS OF TEA)

¼ cup whole cardamom pods

1 teaspoon whole cloves

1 teaspoon black peppercorns

6 cinnamon sticks

⅓ cup cheap black tea leaves (see Note)

1 tablespoon finely diced candied ginger

Sugar, for serving

Whole milk, for serving

In a mortar, grind the cardamom, cloves, peppercorns, and cinnamon sticks with a pestle until everything is roughly ground and fragrant. Stir in the black tea and candied ginger. At this point, you can store it in jars to keep or give away. If intended as a gift, include a little note on how to prepare the tea.

When ready to prepare, for each serving of tea, combine 1 tablespoon tea mixture, 1 teaspoon sugar, ½ cup water, and ½ cup milk in a small saucepan. Heat the liquid to almost boiling, then reduce the heat and let simmer for 4 minutes. (If you like a less robust tea, simmer for just 2 to 3 minutes.) Strain the tea through a fine-mesh sieve into warmed teacup(s).

note It's best to use a lesser-quality black tea, such as Twinings, PG Tips, or any other form of inexpensive loose-leaf tea. The finer grind of the tea leaves in these cheaper teas brews stronger and more consistent with the *chai wallahs* (tea vendors) of Southern India. Reserve your high end, uncut loose-leaf tea for a different use.

Everyone should experience the joy of making their own stove-top popcorn from scratch. Once you realize how delicious and easy it is to make, I promise you'll never go back to those microwave powdered chemicals again. Even better, it takes only a matter of minutes and just a handful of ingredients: a small scoop of corn kernels, fat, and a big pot.

Here is a base recipe for making your own batch, then doctoring it up in three different outfits: 1) hippy manna from the heavens, made with Bragg liquid amino acids and nutritional yeast (sounds weird, but it's so good it's BANANAS); 2) a classy version with fresh thyme, Parmesan, and black pepper; and 3) the all-out addictive kettle corn salty-sweet variety made with maple syrup. I cannot pick favorites among my children, so just make them all!

HOMEMADE POPCORN, THREE WAYS

SERVES 2

BASE POPCORN RECIPE

2 tablespoons coconut oil

½ cup popcorn kernels

Topping of choice (recipes follow)

In a large pot, combine the coconut oil and 3 single popcorn kernels. Cover the pot and set over medium heat. As soon as you hear one of those kernels pop, the oil has come to temperature. Pour the remaining ½ cup popcorn kernels into the pot, then immediately cover. Continue to heat for 3 to 5 minutes—when you start to hear popping sounds, agitate the pot by moving it around a little bit on the burner. When the popping sounds dissipate, your popcorn is done (you may have a few little kernels left, but that's okay). Pour the popcorn into a large bowl and toss with one of the toppings.

note All these varieties of popcorn will stay pretty crisp if stored in an airtight container for a few days.

MAPLE KETTLE CORN

You'll need to gather your ingredients before popping your corn, as you add the maple syrup and the sugar to the hot oil. In addition to the coconut oil and popcorn kernels, you'll need:

2 tablespoons maple syrup

1 tablespoon sugar

2 teaspoons smoked salt

Right when the test kernels have popped and you're ready to add the full amount of popcorn to the hot oil, add the maple syrup and sugar as well. Shake the pot a little more often as the kernels pop, so the sugar doesn't pool together, and be sure to remove the pot before you can smell the sugar starting to scorch. (You're looking for that fine line between caramelized and burned sugar, and it's prudent to cut your losses and take the pot off the stove before the sugar is blackened, even if that means a few extra unpopped kernels.)

Pour the finished popcorn immediately into a large bowl and sprinkle the smoked salt over the top, shaking your bowl a few times to distribute. Serve warm.

BRAGG/NUTRITIONAL YEAST TOPPING

2 tablespoons unsalted butter

1 tablespoon Bragg liquid aminos (or soy sauce if you're in a pinch)

¼ cup nutritional yeast

In a small saucepan, melt the butter. Pour the melted butter as evenly as possible over the top of the popcorn. Pour the liquid aminos on next and give the whole thing a good stir. Sprinkle the nutritional yeast all over and stir to combine. Serve warm.

THYME, PEPPER & PARMESAN TOPPING

2 tablespoons unsalted butter

2 teaspoons fresh thyme leaves, very finely chopped

1 teaspoon freshly ground black pepper

¼ cup grated Parmesan cheese

In a small saucepan, melt the butter. Pour the melted butter as evenly as possible over the top of the popcorn. Sprinkle evenly with the thyme, black pepper, and Parmesan. Give the bowl a few shakes to let the spices and cheese settle into the popcorn crevices. Serve warm.

SWEET & SALTY PUMPKIN SEED CLUSTERS

SERVES 4

1 cup pumpkin seeds

2 tablespoons honey

2 tablespoons sugar

1 teaspoon ground cinnamon

¼ teaspoon freshly grated nutmeg

¼ teaspoon ground ginger

Pinch of ground cloves

½ teaspoon fine sea salt

I find it sad that pumpkin seeds, or pepitas as they're known in many Spanish-speaking parts of the world, are often relegated to a one-day, post-Halloween cooking event. I want to eat sweet, salty, spiced pepitas all year long, and they're an unsung ingredient in a lot of my favorite recipes. Everyone should have the experience of roasting hulled pumpkin seeds at least once in their life. As these are roasting, your kitchen transforms into a cozy realm of autumnal flavor. You can practically hear the crunch of dry leaves and feel the crisp chill of the season! And once the cooking is done, you have a dead-easy, highly addictive little bite in about 20 minutes, great for garnishing soups and salads.

Preheat the oven to 350°F. Line a rimmed baking sheet with parchment paper or a silicone baking mat.

In a medium bowl, toss together the pumpkin seeds, honey, sugar, cinnamon, nutmeg, ginger, cloves, and salt until everything is thoroughly combined. Spread the mixture onto the prepared baking sheet and bake for 15 minutes, rotating the pan front to back halfway through the cooking time, for even browning.

Let the pumpkin seeds cool completely before breaking into clusters. Package in a sealed jar or bag for gifting. Can be kept for up to 1 week in a sealed container.

SPICED MANGO BUTTER

MAKES 1½ CUPS

I whizzed up this condiment seeking something more exciting than the flavor of store-bought ketchup. I still wanted something silky, smooth, and easy to eat; truth be told, I was seeking the ideal jammy butter for dipping a veg cutlet (page 98) into—a sweet chutney akin to what I've enjoyed all over India and Southeast Asia. But what I wound up with was worlds better than what I imagined. Here we have a gently spiced sweet, sour, and savory sauce that complements everything. Tucked into a grilled cheese, spread with butter on biscuits, swirled into grains with tons of fresh herbs, or next to a seared pork chop, it earns a place in every single dish.

1 tablespoon coconut oil

½ medium onion, diced

1½ teaspoons minced fresh ginger

¼ teaspoon freshly ground black pepper

¼ teaspoon chili powder

¼ teaspoon ground cloves

¼ teaspoon ground cumin

⅛ teaspoon ground cardamom

¼ cup packed light brown sugar

1 tablespoon lemon juice

1 teaspoon tomato paste

2 small mangoes, roughly chopped (about 2¼ cups)

In a large skillet, melt the coconut oil over medium-high heat. Add the onion and cook until slightly soft, 3 to 4 minutes. Add the ginger, pepper, chili powder, cloves, cumin, and cardamom. Stir to evenly coat the onion in the spice mixture and cook for another minute.

Add the brown sugar, lemon juice, tomato paste, and chopped mangoes and stir to coat. Cook the fruit, stirring constantly, until slightly softened when pressed with the back of a spoon, 5 to 8 minutes.

Remove the pan from the heat and transfer the mango mixture to a bowl. Let cool to room temperature. Pour the mixture into a blender and puree until smooth. Scoop the butter into sealable glass containers and keep in the fridge until ready to use—it will last for about 1 week.

Kale Pesto

LEFT: Spiced Mango Butter
MIDDLE: Kale Pesto, *page 201*
RIGHT: Onion Jam, *page 200*

This onion jam is so good, I would happily marry a jarful of it, given how many of my favorite foods it complements. It was the first of many edible joys I learned to make at the stove of Adrian Hale, stellar food stylist, inquisitive food writer, frequent collaborator, and dear friend. Now I'm her star onion jam pupil, since I make it so frequently. I sneak spoonfuls of it as I stand in front of the fridge while contemplating dinner; I generously top morning toasts with it. Add a thin shaving of hard cheese and it's like enjoying a bowl of French onion soup in tartine form. And definitely mix this jam into a bubbling pot of savory oats, jasmine rice, or even atop a platter of braised greens. There's no meal that cannot be improved upon with a punch of this caramelly onion jam.

ONION JAM

MAKES ABOUT 1 CUP

2 tablespoons olive oil

2 medium onions, thinly sliced

½ medium Fuji or Granny Smith apple, peeled and grated

Leaves from 2 sprigs fresh rosemary, chopped

2 teaspoons fine sea salt

¼ teaspoon freshly ground black pepper

¼ cup white wine

1 bay leaf

2 tablespoons sugar

1 teaspoon white wine vinegar (optional)

1 tablespoon unsalted butter (optional)

In a large Dutch oven, heat the olive oil over medium heat. Add the onions, apple, rosemary, salt, and pepper and cook, stirring often, until the onions are wilted and coated in oil, about 10 minutes. When the onions start to turn translucent, add the wine and bay leaf and cover. Reduce the heat to medium-low and cook until the onions are softened and turning golden, about 20 minutes, stirring about every 10 minutes.

Uncover and discard the bay leaf. Reduce the heat to low and add ¼ cup water and the sugar. Stir and let the mixture start to slowly take on color as it cooks for 1 hour—you'll need to stir the jam every 10 to 15 minutes to make sure it's not getting too brown in any one place. If the mixture sticks to the pot but is still not browned, add another ¼ cup water and stir as needed, until the entire mixture is thick and deeply amber and fragrant. If desired, stir in the vinegar and butter. Taste one last time to check seasonings.

When sealed in a glass jar, the jam will keep for up to 2 weeks in the fridge.

KALE PESTO

MAKES 1¾ CUPS

I love the bright, bracing flavor of kale, so I tried my hand at blitzing it into a pesto. Now I'm a convert. Spread onto toast, tossed with warm pasta, mixed into a grain salad, or dolloped onto roasted sweet potatoes, kale pesto can ramp up a plain dish. There's a nice bitterness at work that the more ubiquitous basil pesto simply lacks; here the strong, raw greens are tempered by the Parmesan cheese, raw pistachios, and plenty of good-quality olive oil, with a few basil leaves for balance.

---

1 bunch kale, stems removed (about 4 cups roughly chopped leaves)

2 garlic cloves, minced

1 cup pistachios

¼ cup fresh basil leaves

½ cup olive oil, plus more for the container

¼ cup lemon juice

½ teaspoon fine sea salt, plus more for seasoning

Freshly ground black pepper

1 cup grated Parmesan cheese

In a food processor, combine the kale, garlic, pistachios, basil, olive oil, lemon juice, salt, and pepper to taste. Process on high speed until the mixture is smooth. If you need to loosen the texture, add a teaspoon or two of water and continue to process. Add the Parmesan and blend until fully incorporated. Taste for seasonings and add more salt and pepper to taste.

Place in a small bowl or glass jar, cover the top with a thin layer of olive oil, seal, and refrigerate for up to 5 days. This pesto freezes well in small containers or plastic bags, and it keeps for up to 1 month.

LABNEH BALLS

MAKES ABOUT 12

Labneh is a form of Middle Eastern yogurt cheese, delicious when smeared atop crostini, tucked into savory pancakes, or enjoyed alongside any roasted fruit. But while it's highly versatile, perhaps its most delicious application is by itself, lightly rolled in various spices and packed in oil.

---

1 container (32 ounces) plain whole-milk Greek yogurt (4 cups)

1 teaspoon fine sea salt

Olive oil, for drizzling and preserving the yogurt balls

3 tablespoons dried thyme

3 tablespoons ground paprika

3 tablespoons ground cumin

In a medium bowl, mix together the yogurt and salt. Line a sieve with a folded piece of cheesecloth and place the sieve over a deep bowl (make sure there is enough room in the bowl to catch the whey without submerging the sieve). Spoon the yogurt into the sieve and let drain in the fridge for 36 hours, until the consistency is very thick. Discard the whey.

At this point you can serve as is, with a drizzle of olive oil. For something a little fancier, shape into small balls, about 1 tablespoon of labneh each (the aged labneh will be stiff enough to hold a ball shape), and leave them uncovered on a tray in the fridge for 12 hours, until they have slightly dried out.

Spread the dried thyme, paprika, and cumin out on their own plate. Roll each labneh ball in one of the spices and place in a jar, creating a variety of yogurt balls with a range of spices in the jar. Cover the balls with olive oil and keep in the fridge until ready to eat. These herbed balls will keep up to 1 month.

note One of these luscious orbs, dripping with flavor and juiciness, can elevate a simple salad or mezze platter into a thing of beauty.

thanks

This book is the result of an amazing team of friends, colleagues, and family members cheering me along and supporting me through this exciting, challenging process. I'd like to have you all over for a raucous dessert picnic at the beach in Santa Barbara one day. Please know you're already invited. I'll bring the chocolate sandwiches.

A very heartfelt thank-you to my agent, Betsy Amster, who e-mailed me years ago after seeing a photo of me in a pink floral bathrobe making hot chocolate on TheKitchn.com. It's with her unwavering confidence in me and expertise in the field that you now hold this book in your hands. Thank you to Jessica Freeman Slade, the editor who acquired this project, and to Angelin Borsics, who took over midway and helped me finish and usher it into the world. To La Tricia Watford for her beautiful design, and to the rest of the Clarkson Potter team for making my book the best it could be: Doris Cooper, Aaron Wehner, Heather Williamson, Joyce Wong, Kevin Sweeting, and Sean Boyles.

I was fortunate enough to have Ayda Robana style the food and drinks for this book. Ayda, you breathed life, color, and beauty into all of my food, and for that I'll be forever grateful. To Adrian Hale, Deena Prichep, and Roxanne Rosensteel, for testing and retesting all of the recipes we've gathered here. Your palates, food knowledge, hard work, and enthusiasm for eating exceptionally inspired me every day we worked together. I hope we all get to feast at the same table soon.

My life and my book would be remiss if not for Teja Ream and Kate Perlis. You two are my oldest friends and helped me shape this project, with our lifetime of tea parties, backyard snacks, and shared joys.

To my parents, Richard and Cissy, who taught me that good food, strong friendships, faraway travel, and reaching for my dreams are not only possible, but they are also essential. And to my brother, Nick, who is the exceptional cook in my family—the person who menu-plans each weekend and manages to create inventive, delicious meals fit for his queen, Kelly.

Last, and certainly most, thank you to my husband, David Kilpatrick. You are my collaborator in all things, and this book is no exception. Having you at my side while I cooked, wrote, styled, danced, and photographed my way through this project has been the biggest buoy of all. Your encouragement and help with every aspect of this book made me feel like the sparkliest author there ever was.

Index